Using
Intensive
Interaction
with a Person
with a Social or
Communicative
Impairment

of related interest

Understanding Intensive Interaction
Context and Concepts for Professionals and Families
Graham Firth, Ruth Berry and Cath Irvine
Foreword by Dave Hewett
ISBN 978 1 84310 982 2

Promoting Social Interaction for Individuals with Communicative Impairments
Making Contact
Edited by M. Suzanne Zeedyk
ISBN 978 1 84310 539 8

Using
Intensive
Interaction
with a Person
with a Social or
Communicative
Impairment

Graham Firth and Mark Barber

Jessica Kingsley *Publishers*
London and Philadelphia

First published in 2011
by Jessica Kingsley Publishers
116 Pentonville Road
London N1 9JB, UK
and
400 Market Street, Suite 400
Philadelphia, PA 19106, USA

www.jkp.com

Library of Congress Cataloging in Publication Data
A CIP catalog record for this book is available from the Library of Congress

British Library Cataloguing in Publication Data
A CIP catalogue record for this book is available from the British Library

ISBN 978 1 84905 109 5

Printed and bound in Great Britain by
MPG Books Group Limited

CONTENTS

PREFACE 9

INTRODUCTION   **11**

What is Intensive Interaction? 11

Who might benefit from Intensive Interaction? 13

Why should you be considering using Intensive Interaction? 14

Who else may you need to talk to about using Intensive Interaction? . .15

CHAPTER 1 What to Do and Think About Before Using
Intensive Interaction   **19**

Where are you going to try to use Intensive Interaction – is this
the best place? 19

What kind of observation have you done with the person – is it
enough? 21

What are you going to try to achieve in the first few minutes? 26

What are you hoping to achieve in the whole session? 28

Is this the best time to try and start – does it have to be now? 30

How long have you got – is it going to be long enough? 31

Do you have any necessary resource items available? 34

CHAPTER 2 What to Do and Think About While Using
Intensive Interaction   **39**

What can you do to engage someone – what techniques can you use? 39

Thinking back to your observations – what have you learned, and
what should you be looking for now? 46

How do you know if the person is ready for Intensive Interaction? . . .51

Is this the best time to try and start – does it have to be now? 53

How do you approach the person – what do you do first? 55

What should you be looking for as you go along? 58

Do you always have to follow the other person's lead, or are there
times when you can lead the activity in some way? 64

Have you achieved what you hoped for so far – what responses
 have you had, and were these what you were expecting or not? 66

Are you still being sufficiently observant of the person? 69

This particular activity has been going on for quite a long time –
 should you change what you are doing or just keep going?. 70

What are you hoping to achieve in the whole session? 72

How much direct mirroring should you be doing – and how
 creative can you be with this? 74

What if the person gets bored of repeated routines – how would
 you recognise this and what could you do about it? 75

Can you try something a little different to see how the person
 responds – if so, when and how, and what should it be? 79

Do you still have the necessary resource items available?. 82

How will you know if you have achieved something worthwhile? 83

How long have you got left – is it going to be long enough? 84

How do you disengage with the person if it is going well and
 they really want to continue? 85

Should Intensive Interaction be this easy or this hard? 86

CHAPTER 3 What to Do and Think About After Using
Intensive Interaction   91

What did you do to engage the person – what techniques did you
 use and what have you learned from this session? 91

How did you know if the person was ready for Intensive
 Interaction, and was this a good time to start a session? 95

How did you approach the person – what did you do first, and
 how was this received?. 96

What new behaviours did you observe from the person during
 this session? 100

Did you achieve what you hoped for, and was it worthwhile? 103

Were you sufficiently observant of the person? Did they, or might
 they have done something you didn't see?. 105

Could you use some different resource items to better effect next
 time?. 107

Did you have long enough?. 109

How did you disengage with the person? 110

What was easy or hard about the session? .112

CHAPTER 4 Some Final Issues to Consider When Using
Intensive Interaction   115

Consider what you can do to develop your own competence and
confidence as an Intensive Interaction practitioner 115

Consider how other people can be productively involved and
supported in developing successful Intensive Interaction 120

Consider how Intensive Interaction can be used in the longer
term, and how this issue is best addressed and organised 128

CHAPTER 5 What You Might Expect to Come From the Use
of Intensive Interaction   133

FURTHER READING 137

GLOSSARY 141

APPENDIX: RECORDING SHEETS FOR INTENSIVE INERACTION . . .147

REFERENCES 153

INDEX 157

PREFACE

This book focuses on helping the reader, whether they are parents, carers, teachers, support staff or therapists, to find a range of ways of connecting interactively with a person who has a severe social or communicative impairment. The book is set out the way it is to help the reader progressively support their efforts at social interaction and promote a deeper understanding of the practical use of Intensive Interaction. It is also our intention, as the authors, to encourage the reflective practices which are vital to the use of this approach.

Each chapter and section provides you, the reader, with advice about how to approach and undertake the various stages of practice that make up a fully developed Intensive Interaction intervention. For ease of use, the sections are often subdivided further into advice for working interactively with either people who are 'familiar', and those who are 'unfamiliar' and therefore new to you, and there is sometimes an additional section covering 'any other issues' that we feel are worthy of consideration – this format is repeated through the different sections.

The book is not intended to be read in one sitting, but to be read gradually, section by section over time, to extend and eventually build a more comprehensive and practical understanding of the approach. We acknowledge that some of the language used may be new to some readers, so to avoid confusion we have provided a glossary of terms at the back of the book to ensure that our meaning is not confused.

There are some recurrent themes that necessarily reappear several times across different sections of this book, and this is intentional – as Plato said 'the greater part of instruction is being reminded of things you already know'. Therefore the reader will need to be prepared for some issues to reappear and this is because good Intensive Interaction practice is a deliberate and continuous cycle of well-informed observation, actual one to one interaction, and subsequent insightful reflection. This is all then combined with liberal amounts of optimistic perseverance – before, during and after the practical work!

So, this book should be seen as a tool to enhance practice development and constructive reflection among current practitioners of Intensive Interaction. We hope that it will be a useful source of meaningful knowledge and sensible advice which progressively guides and ultimately improves your practice. We wrote the book to be an accessible resource that can be frequently and repeatedly dipped into as you develop your practice and reflective skills over time, and subsequently gain confidence in the approach and in yourself as an Intensive Interaction practitioner. We hope that you find the book useful.

Graham Firth and Mark Barber

Introduction

What is Intensive Interaction?

Imagine you arrive at a cocktail party where you know nobody except the host who introduces you to someone then immediately walks off to attend to other guests. What do you do in this situation? Once any greetings are over, conversations tend to start by the two participants asking general questions of each other to establish some sort of common ground: gentle enquiries about jobs, pastimes and possible connections usually open up enough commonalities to develop a convivial conversation based on any shared interests or preferences.

Intensive Interaction follows a similar path: two people finding common ground, which leads to a communicative exchange where both participants explore each other's preferences and interests. However, Intensive Interaction usually occurs between a more skilled communication partner and someone who is still learning about communication and interaction with another person. In this context the 'beginning communicator' (usually someone with a social or communicative impairment) is supported to express their interests, while the skilled communication partner uses their experience to base the conversation or interaction on the interests and pastimes that the other person indicates.

Intensive Interaction is actually interactive and sociable interplay, where the skilled partner responds to the person with a social or communicative impairment in a manner which helps the interaction to continue and progress. Without claiming to present a final or ultimate definition of the approach, and not wishing to revisit work that already exists in the Intensive Interaction literature, Intensive Interaction can perhaps best be described as a practical and accessible means of achieving social engagement and interaction with people who exhibit a severe social or communicative impairment, which usually, although not always, is the result of a severe or profound and multiple learning disability and/or autistic spectrum disorder (Nind and Hewett 1994).

In more prosaic terms, Intensive Interaction can be viewed as a particular type of conversation between two people, the content of that conversation being negotiated between the participants, so that both parties are empowered to be equal contributors to it. The approach is also a way for finding a connection with someone who is difficult-to-reach, and then building a more equitable and inclusive relationship with them (Firth, Berry and Irvine 2010).

Intensive Interaction can be seen as an educational or developmental method to enable people who experience severe or profound intellectual and multiple disabilities to learn the fundamental elements of social communication and interaction (Nind and Hewett 1994). Doctors Dave Hewett and Melanie Nind, the teachers who in the 1980s carried out the original research and published the first treatise setting out the theory and practice of Intensive Interaction, describe Intensive Interaction as '…an approach to teaching and spending time with people with learning disabilities, which is aimed specifically at the development of the most fundamental social and communication abilities' (Nind and Hewett 2001).

The use of Intensive Interaction can have a number of major aims: genuine and participatory social inclusion, communicative skill acquisition or development, and in some cases therapeutic support. Interestingly, the strategies or techniques underpinning Intensive Interaction do not actually change within these different identifiable purposes. The strategies involved tend to be based on those communication techniques used spontaneously within infant-caregiver interactions (Nind and Hewett 2005, pp.16–17), and are skills or abilities that almost all of us possess at some level and usually practice (and practise) very naturally in our dealings with most pre-verbal people that we meet in our everyday lives, that is, any young infants who we know. Indeed, a very similar and contemporaneous approach to promoting the same type of interactivity was called *Augmented Mothering* (Ephraim 1986), which promoted the continuation of 'mothering' type activities with adults with severe or profound and multiple learning difficulties to foster improved communication and relationship building.

What a practitioner actually does when using Intensive Interaction, that is, the strategies used, will vary depending on the individual characteristics and interests of the two people involved, just as the content of any conversation will vary with different participants. The generally accepted means of achieving Intensive Interaction are those described in *Access to Communication* (Nind and Hewett 1994, 2005), and are termed the *Fundamentals of Communication* (FoC) which typically include:

- sharing personal space

- exchanging eye contacts

- exchanging vocalisations with meaning (for some, speech development)

- engaging in sequences of activity with another person

- taking turns in exchanges of behaviour

- exchanging facial expressions

- exchanging sociable physical contacts

- enjoying being with another person

- giving attention to another person.

As well as the considerations listed above, there is an over-arching methodology that should support the application or use of the approach. Initially, there should be 'mutual pleasure' while engaging in Intensive Interaction (Nind and Hewett 1994, 2005). Moreover, practitioners should ascribe some level of communicative intentionality (Nind and Hewett 1994, 2005) to the actions of the person with an intellectual disability, even if such 'intentionality' is not obviously present (e.g. when someone makes non-symbolic noises, apparently for their own entertainment or stimulation). Finally, the social exchange should be carried forward in a 'taskless way' (Nind and Hewett 1994, 2005), that is, the outcome of the interaction should not be seen as an important consideration; success should be seen in terms of the level of involvement in the process achieved by the person with a social or communicative impairment.

Who might benefit from Intensive Interaction?

When initially developed, in a school that lay within the grounds of a large residential hospital for people who were then described as having a 'mental handicap', Intensive Interaction was developed with a view to addressing the learning needs of people who had severe or profound intellectual disabilities, a significant number of whom also had an additional diagnosis of autism. The students at this school were still at the earliest developmental stages of communication, and the use of the emerging approach was intended to facilitate their learning of the Fundamentals of Communication (Nind and Hewett 1994, 2005).

Currently, Intensive Interaction is seen more broadly as a tool for developing the sociability and early communication skills of people from a number of different groups who have a severe social or communication impairment. Such a social or communication impairment may be the result of a number of causal factors, such as the degree of a person's intellectual impairment, for example a severe or profound intellectual and/or multiple disability; a degenerative neurological condition, for example during the latter stages of dementia (Astell and Ellis 2006); autistic spectrum disorder (ASD); or a socially impoverished infancy, for example due to the child having an 'institutionalised' early upbringing (Zeedyk *et al.* 2009)

Intensive Interaction is also used with people who engage in a variety of self-involved or self-stimulatory activities which can preclude social involvement with other people. It has also been seen to have application with people who experience severe multi-sensory impairments and who, for a number of reasons, may have become severely socially isolated or seem entirely unmotivated or unable to engage in social activity.

Why should you be considering using Intensive Interaction?

Generally, Intensive Interaction has been seen as an approach for providing people with experiences of being socially included and emotionally connected. It also provides people with opportunities to practise and develop the necessary skills to be social, and thus learn about being a social agent in the company of other people.

Increasingly, Intensive Interaction is being seen as a therapeutic tool to use with people who find emotional expression and relationship building to be problematic. In this capacity, the approach appears to address the person's sense of connectedness and self-esteem through a combined process of improved communication and relationship building (Berry in Firth *et al.*, 2010, p.88).

Intensive Interaction can also be successfully used with people who have already developed some degree of symbolic speech and understanding, but whom it is thought might still benefit from being supported to develop their 'fundamental' understanding of the complexities of human communication and social interactivity.

Who else may you need to talk to about using Intensive Interaction?

Any use of Intensive Interaction that successfully promotes learning and increases the social inclusion of people with communicative or social impairments should, as a matter of course, be shared with all the other significant people in that person's life. If means are found to promote sociable interactivity then it is the authors' view that we are morally bound to include as many people in that process as possible. A collaborative approach among those involved is always beneficial, as it increases the number of potential opportunities for interaction and identifies consistent and appropriate practices. Collaboration also promotes discussion and assists in the identification of the best ways to support the process of social inclusion.

First and foremost in such a collaborative or collective approach to the use of Intensive Interaction will be the person's family, especially their parents, primary carers and other family members and carers. Indeed, for a long-term, sustainable implementation of Intensive Interaction, close family members or primary carers should be central to any use of the approach, as they will generally be the most constant and attendant factors in the person's life. The involvement of families and carers is especially vital during periods of transition in the person's life, for example between children's and adult services or between residential placements or respite services. If we involve family members or primary carers, if available, then we are more likely to have a lasting impact on the way people will work and socialise with that person.

Occasionally the use of Intensive Interaction will contrast with, or contradict, the predominant style of working with individual clients in some settings. This may make it difficult for the person with a social or communicative impairment to work out how they can successfully socially initiate or respond to people in their social environment. Inconsistency in such a situation will certainly dilute the impact of any Intensive Interaction, and it might even be confusing if the person comes to value and even expect a certain sociable response, and is at times disappointed by the lack of such a response for reasons that they can not understand.

Ideally, everyone who might have regular contact with the person should be involved in (at least employing) any successful Intensive Interaction strategies. This involves teachers or educational support assistants and allied colleagues. Indeed, quite often it might be that an Intensive Interaction intervention initially comes from such a source, as the approach was originally seen as an educational intervention and is used within many special schools, further education (TAFE in Australia) provision or even some day service environments. Again, if it is possible to work consistently and supportively together any potential benefits to the person should be increased and more certainly realised.

It is always wise to involve other Intensive Interaction practitioners in your setting for their general support and advice, especially if they have extended experience of using the approach. The contributions of other Intensive Interaction practitioners can be of great help in terms of engaging in reflective discussions on aspects of your practice or helping in the analysis of any video recordings taken. Having a supportive group of fellow practitioners who are capable of giving encouraging, honest and insightful feedback on your Intensive Interaction practice can be an invaluable resource for reflection and supervision. Such a supervisory or support network will also provide added confidence in any Intensive Interaction that takes place, as the combined experiences of such a group or network can advise on the potential ways to move forward. Support is also invaluable for isolated practitioners who are facing difficulties with colleagues or find themselves in conflict with the dominant styles of practices in their workplace.

It is to be hoped that other concerned or involved professionals, such as speech and language therapists, clinical psychologists, or occupational therapists (and others, such as supportive music therapists), can be called upon to help sustain and inform an Intensive Interaction intervention. If you work formally, or even informally as a multi-disciplinary team around the person who might benefit from Intensive Interaction, you are more likely to succeed than if you work in isolation and potentially in conflict with each other. Intensive Interaction should ideally be used as part of a comprehensive individual care package or Individual Educational Plan (IEP) that brings together all the necessary approaches that are required to support the person to enjoy their life, and realise their potential in terms of sociable interconnection and inclusion.

Finally, if we wish the person to be more successfully included across a wider social network, it is important that anyone with regular contact with the person becomes familiar with the idiosyncratic ways that they communicate and explore social interactions. Over time, transport or escort staff – even the people at the corner shop – could be encouraged to be involved.

CHAPTER 1 What to Do and Think About Before Using Intensive Interaction

Where are you going to try to use Intensive Interaction – is this the best place?

When working with a person who is unfamiliar to you

It is certainly best practice to observe the person quite closely before actually trying to engage with them, as, if you want to take the cocktail party analogy mentioned earlier, it is best to have a good idea of the sort of conversational starter you might try to use with them. An important aspect of these initial observations involves noting where the person likes to spend time:

- Do they have a favourite place to be?

- Do they sit in the same place most of the time?

- Do they like space? How much?

- Do they like to be near a wall?

- Do they seem more relaxed sitting on the floor?

- Where do they spend their time when nobody is trying to direct them? Do they select quiet places away from other people?

Look for the person's regular haunts: some people might wander around the room, but they may pause in certain places; or they may scan the room when standing in a particular area. There may be certain times within a sequence of wandering, especially if that wandering follows a predicable pattern, where eye contact or even your close proximity is acceptable to them. As you initially try to engage or interact with the person, you might stand near a place used for pauses, or you might situate yourself in easy view of a favourite position for scanning the room.

When you are choosing the place to engage the person initially, it is worthwhile considering the person's hearing and sight – consider if there is confusing or poor lighting or lots of competing and possibly distracting noises. You will get the best idea of where to interact by watching where the person frequently chooses to be when undirected or during a break or recess. In schools, the choice of where to interact is often influenced by the requirement not to be alone in a room with a person. Experience tells us that in a structured setting like schools, recess (or lunch/playtime) is often the best time to try to engage with the person initially. Recess is frequently a time of less focused activity and socialising, making it a perfect and public setting to demonstrate good interactive practice in front of colleagues.

When working with a person who is familiar to you

If the person is independently mobile and you are familiar to them, then you can place yourself where they generally like to be. Alternatively you might wait until you see the person in their familiar place and settled there, to watch for their focus of attention before going to them. It is a good rule to make yourself available where the person is, rather than to expect him or her to come to you. If you do physically approach the person, it is important that you do not 'crowd' them and that you move in such a way that they can easily withdraw from any exchange if they wish.

Other issues that you may need to consider

If the person you are going to work with has visual or hearing impairments, it might be sensible to begin in quieter areas to ensure that they have a chance of noticing your responses to their activity. But bear in mind that to be sustainable, it is always best to interact with someone in familiar contexts.

When working with people who cannot move independently, an important part of your initial observation should involve noticing how relaxed they are in the setting in which they find themselves.

Be mindful that they probably had no control over where they were placed, prior to you beginning your observation. Questions you might ask yourself might include:

- Are they showing signs of defensiveness or amusement?

- Are they curious, wary or uninterested in the activities surrounding them?

- Are they responding to elements of the noises or the proximity of people nearby?

- Do you need to put out mats or fetch a hoist? Before working with someone, find out how long they have been in their wheelchair prior to your arrival. If they need a break from sitting, you can always interact on mats. Use hoists or seek support from nearby staff to assist you. *Always* use approved manual handling techniques and *never* lift alone!

- Are there any contextual/environmental issues you need to address? For example, are there any trip hazards for ambulant people, choking hazards with resource items, etc.?

- Will the other people in the room be somehow affected by any Intensive Interaction? Will you need to do something about this?

What kind of observation have you done with the person – is it enough?

When working with a person who is unfamiliar to you

When is enough ever enough? The purpose of observation is to identify some of what the person you are going to work with finds interesting or attractive. When you begin doing Intensive Interaction with a person, the first stages involve finding common ground with them – just like your first meeting with anyone. Initial contact is largely made up of gentle social probing aimed at identifying a focus which both partners can happily share. When working with clients with significant intellectual disabilities, however, this process often does not have the luxury of words to help the process along. The skilled partner observes the person to identify their preferred mode of activity. One of the observation schedules in the appendix might help you place some structure on your observation and give it some direction.

Ideally, you should observe the person for at least 15 minutes on at least three different occasions. It can be beneficial to make the observations at different times of the day. To ensure that what you are watching is the person's own agenda, rather than their efforts to conform to someone else's, it is perhaps best to make some observations when the person is not being supported or included in a social activity. Watching someone involved in something which interests them can tell you a lot about where they like to be; the speed at which they naturally behave; pauses they naturally take; what sort of activities they enjoy; the qualities of any objects that interest them; or the type of touch they use.

Observation will also provide information on the types of behaviour the person uses to give themselves a feeling of being an active agent, the level of repetition or uniformity with which they investigate the same or similar sensations, and importantly whether they enjoy social activity or spontaneously address any behaviour to others.

The process of observation provides the skilled partner with foreknowledge of the range of behaviours the person is likely to recognise or be interested in when they happen somewhere else. Watching the person, the practitioner should be considering which of their activities they might be able to respond to, in a way which might open up an interaction, and what they (the skilled partner) would do to approach the person to accomplish this. It is likely that, if your initial attempt to engage the person is based on what you have seen them doing for its own sake, they will recognise what you are doing – that is, you will find common ground.

- The person does something, then pauses…
- You do something recognisably related to it, stopping when you see the person restart…
- The person acts again…
- You respond again…

Even though the person might be initially involved in an activity for its own satisfaction, say twirling an object in front of their eyes, or rhythmically tapping onto a chair arm or vocalising in a particular way, or perhaps they do something simply because they can, at some point they might act and then watch to see if your reaction responds to or somehow mirrors their activity.

When working with someone who, because of the complex nature of their physical disabilities, has a very limited range of movement, it might be necessary to note any sounds that they make (even breathing sounds, sighs, lip-smacks or wheezes), or sensations they repeatedly generate, to inform how you are going to respond. People can also recognise someone else making the same lip-smacks or wheezes that they make, and they may well respond by producing the sound more frequently to check if your sounds respond to theirs (or by 'stilling', presumably to see if your sound also stops).

In some circumstances it might also be necessary to talk to direct carers before starting any observations, and this will be necessary if the person with a social or communicative impairment also has a potential to engage in any challenging behaviours. Talking to carers in such instances means that you can avoid doing anything that might put yourself, or others, or the person themselves at risk of any physical harm. It will also be useful to gather some basic information about how the person might express their emotional state, and it is important to remember that these ways may be counter-intuitive (e.g. they may laugh when they are anxious not when they are happy) or their expressions may be very subtle (e.g. indicating anxiety through increased respiration rates). Given that the way a person's mood manifests itself will probably be very idiosyncratic, it might be best to discuss what happiness, anxiety, pleasure, etc. 'looks like' in this person, with someone who has known them for longer than you.

After observing a person who is unfamiliar to you, there will come a time when you wish to start interacting with the person, and you will need to ask yourself if your observations have been sufficient to give you a clear idea of where to start. It might be useful to reflect on the following questions when considering whether your observations are sufficient:

- Have you seen the person in more than one place or situation?

- Have you seen the person at different times of the day?

- Have you seen the person when supported by a number of different staff or carers?

A range of observations at different times, in different situations, and with different support staff or carers can suggest a wider range of potential strategies (or topics of conversation) for you to explore together. However, sometimes it can happen that the person initiates an interaction with you as you observe them, and generally it is then best to 'go with the flow' and attempt some kind of interactivity, rather than ignore such attempts at social initiation.

When working with a person who is familiar to you

When working with a person who is familiar to you, you may not need to engage in much prior observation before commencing any Intensive Interaction with them (although you should never become complacent and think that further periods of objective observation will not be of any use – it is not unusual for some people to overestimate how well they know a person simply because they have worked with or cared for that person for an extended period).

However, you still need to make sure that they are comfortable and in an apparently receptive mood, or conversely if they look in some way anxious or upset and are therefore unlikely to be receptive. For people who you are familiar with, you may need to look at their facial expressions, the rhythm or tempo of their physical movements, behaviour or activity, the harshness or inconsistency of their eye contact, and their apparent acceptance, or otherwise, of your proximity. These things might be useful to observe before you commence, and might influence if or how you commence.

If you find yourself inventing new interactive repertoires that are unrelated to the person's agenda, or wondering what the next 'level' of response is, the chances are you need to repeat your observations because you are losing focus on the person and wanting to achieve your own goals. Your responses should always follow what the person is doing, even if you know them really well. Before working with someone, it is advisable to monitor their level of excitement, as well as the focus and the cadence of their activity. That way you know you will be responding at the right speed and the person can then pursue their exploration of what will happen next, at their optimum level of arousal.

Other issues that you may need to consider

Other issues you may wish to observe might be environmental, that is, have you worked with this person in this situation before, and might the environment impose particular constraints on any activity, or might it provide new opportunities?

- Is the sound and lighting suitable, and if not can you adjust them appropriately? Sometimes in certain environments you may wish to use ambient or relaxing music in the background (this can sometimes be helpful if there are auditory distractions from external sources, e.g. cars passing outside, or even from any loud or persistent vocalisations of other people present in the room at the same time).

- Are there other people in the vicinity that might be affected by your attempts at Intensive Interaction? Do they need someone to support them or are they all right as they are?

- Are there any safety issues that might be visible, for example trip hazards for ambulant clients or choking hazards for people who chew or mouth explore objects?

- Are there any health-related issues that you might need to consider, for example colds or flu that are currently prevalent (even possibly hepatitis, MRSA, infectious warts on people's hands, etc.) that might require certain precautions to minimise the spread of infection?

Please note that washing your hands between interactions with different people is always advised, especially if the person has problems containing saliva or any other body fluids. This does not relate specifically to practitioners of Intensive Interaction, but applies to anyone working with a lot of different people. Regular hand washing prevents the distribution of transferable viruses and bacteria.

Whichever group of people you work with, good hygiene practices are invaluable in minimising avoidable infection. Any cuts and grazes on hands should also be covered, then cleaned and aired at the end of the working day.

What are you going to try to achieve in the first few minutes?

When working with a person who is unfamiliar to you

Initially, you (i.e. the communication partner) really need to intrigue the person, or attract their attentional focus, for example from their current, possibly sensory or solitary, focus, towards you or towards an aspect of what you are doing. This can frequently be accomplished by 'using behaviours the person will recognise as their own' (Bowen 2007; also Caldwell 2002).

Any first contact can be fleeting; the reaction to your approach or action may be very positive but also it might simply be that the person stills, or apparently only momentarily attends to you or what you are doing. It is important not to intrude too much or to impose yourself on their activity. It is sensible to watch them closely for any signs about how the person feels about spending time with you. Remember that in the person's experience, your approach might be quite unusual – indeed they might expect that you are going to take them somewhere or make some requirements of them. You are always working in the shadow of the person's previous experience of exchanges with 'staff' who might not historically have placed much value on the person's agenda. So give the person time to notice that you are responding to them and to their interest.

If the person is anxious at all because of your presence, you should consider how to approach them differently. Leaving some distance between yourself and the person allows them to enter the space near to you if they are interested in exploring you further or interacting with you. This is much more desirable than you approaching the person, or inadvertently entering their space too quickly or intrusively. If it is your approach which disturbs the person, then find the distance at which you are acceptable, and negotiate the distance by backing off when their response tells you that their anxiety is rising. Repeatedly backing off or approaching in response to the person's behaviour demonstrates that you are controllable and responsive. You are still interacting – the conversation is about distance. Most importantly, the person is finding out that other people will respond to their actions.

When working with a person who is familiar to you

When you approach someone who is familiar, the chances are there is already some mutual acknowledgement occurring when you meet. Recognition, curiosity, an approach, or a smile might indicate that the person is interested in being with you. Don't assume or require eye contact, as it can sometimes be emotionally intrusive for people. Once the person has greeted or acknowledged you, they might well enter the space you have left between you. If you enter this space, watch closely for any raised anxiety or defensive reaction. At best, the first few moments may be marked with a recognisable greeting behaviour, or by the person watching what you do in response to what they do.

As a first initiation you might wish to wait until you see the person in their apparently familiar place, engaged in a pattern of behaviour which you have already considered an interactive response to. Alternatively it might be equally fruitful to 'hover' on the periphery of the person's activity, responding interactively to demonstrate your interest in their activity, but waiting for an invitation to join in or get closer. You are looking for a response which confirms that you are on the person's 'intellectual radar' and that they are either quite relaxed about that or quite interested in it.

Other issues that you may need to consider

When working with people with visual and hearing impairments, it is important to prepare them before getting close or touching them. A 'sensory signature' might be used to alert the person to your presence. When working with Claire, who is blind, staff will always use her name and other familiar sounds as they approach her, and before touching her gently. Then, acknowledging that Claire may well have been focusing on internal or sensory events prior to their arrival, they will sit with her for a couple of minutes, stroking her arm, to give her a chance to 'tune in' to their presence. Before continuing with an exchange, they wait for Claire to begin to orient to them, or show signs of her awareness of them.

People with hearing impairments should always be approached taking advantage of knowledge about where you can best be seen by the person as you draw near. You don't want to startle someone in the first few moments of any Intensive Interaction!

What are you hoping to achieve in the whole session?

When working with a person who is unfamiliar to you

The short answer to this often asked question is that it is a mistake to expect to achieve something finite, that is, a goal or predicted outcome in a 'session'. You are offering an opportunity for the person to engage with you – the role of a skilled Intensive Interaction partner is to be responsive and supportive of the person's actions, agendas and potentially communicative acts.

The first time you meet a person you are deliberately behaving in ways that aim to be interesting to them, while trying to find a mutual interest to share your attention with. Like your first meeting with someone who does not experience an intellectual disability, your first exchange will most likely focus on exploring any common ground. Your 'hope for the whole session' is that you might explore this together harmoniously and with mutual pleasure.

As the initial interaction develops, you should be carefully monitoring the patterns of response or repeatedly visited routines that the person visits within any emerging dialogue. These patterns often provide insight into their understanding of what is happening, and their responses to your pauses indicate whether they are anticipating a response to their action. Watching for and responding in kind to the person's interests frequently leads to a situation where they will try to confirm that it is *their* reactions you are responding to. This initial exploration opens up an 'arena for negotiation' where the person begins to develop an awareness of themselves as a social agent in such an exchange.

Your observations have, it is hoped, alerted you to some of the range of behaviours and interests that the person typically demonstrates

– this, then, is the common ground that you should be alert to. Early interactions frequently involve the practitioner following the person's behavioural lead by responding to actions or activity in the pauses left between them. This often leads the person to explore the responses they receive, often by repetition or increased monitoring of the practitioner. These first points of contact may well become the reference points for following interactions and from which playfully ritualised exchanges develop.

When working with a person who is familiar to you

Previous interactions will give you some idea of what to expect, but still, you should enter into interactions without a predetermined outcome in mind. Over time your consistent responses will enable the person to develop familiarity with communicative conventions (e.g. 'my smiles are reciprocated', or 'my outstretched hand is taken and held') or interactive routines and repertoires. Over time, and through repetition, these evolving routines become both established and interconnected allowing the person to move from one to the other.

Depending on how familiar two people are, they might revisit features of previous interactions, either partner might slightly adjust their previous contribution to see whether the other partner recognises and is interested in pursuing this. As long as you stay within the person's frequent and established repertoire, it is quite possible to explore the proverbial 'envelope' of what you might do together. It is likely that the person will be interested, attentive and often amused by you, as long as the nature of the exchange remains both familiar and recognisable.

It is always hoped that the two communication partners can share and acknowledge each other's company, with the skilled partner endeavouring to find the means of developing mutual attunement and enjoyment in each other. However, your main goal is to open up the encounter to enable the person to maintain their involvement in the ebb and flow of a social encounter successfully. You should be making no judgements about the quality of a response; neither should you be requiring standard or conventionally recognised responses. You should be accepting and clearly acknowledging the person's natural responses in a manner which encourages further contributions. Like a tennis coach and a novice, the coach always plays the ball into a place in the person's court where they will find it easy to reach and comfortable to hit it back, using the skills they are developing.

Other issues that you may need to consider

Sometimes you may have other people present and observing your sessions of Intensive Interaction, and they might have opinions, and possible predetermined ideas, about what ought to be achieved. Sometimes just having such people present (e.g. educational or social care inspectors, senior managers or head teachers, visiting dignitaries or interested professionals) can generate a pressure on you to be seen to 'achieve' something tangible during an Intensive Interaction session. Such pressure should be resisted, and time taken beforehand to enlighten people who observe from the outside (and who sometimes make influential, although not always well informed judgements on the interactions before them) about the approach and the rationale that supports it.

However a good rule of thumb is – if you are worried about what other people are thinking about you when engaging in Intensive Interaction, then you aren't concentrating enough on the person you're interacting with.

Is this the best time to try and start – does it have to be now?

When working with a person who is unfamiliar to you

'Why not now?' is certainly a good question to ask. You should certainly make yourself aware of any appropriate reasons not to proceed, but it is probably the best policy to approach someone, or allow them to approach you, with the presumption that now is the best time to start – unless there is visible evidence to the contrary.

Obviously you should not force someone to be interactive if they aren't going to be voluntarily receptive to it, and so you should be sensitive to any signs of raised anxiety, or signs of tiredness, or an obvious wish to engage in some other available activity, for example eating or drinking! But you should generally proceed with a sensitive optimism that now is all right for Intensive Interaction.

When working with a person who is familiar to you

Depending on how familiar you are with the person, and on how focused they are on their own activity, it might be fruitful for you to suggest a 'game' (or 'format') that relates to an established or recently enjoyed interaction. This approach might be interesting and lead to a new conversation. However, if it is not all right, then you can simply revert to responding to the activity that the person was involved with previously when you approached them, or the activity that they are currently focused on or involved in now.

Other issues that you may need to consider

'Do you genuinely have enough time?' might be a question worth considering. 'Is there something else that is likely to happen in five minutes that will terminate any developed interactivity?' If so, you may decide it is better to arrange for another time when you might have longer to engage the person. Although for some people five minutes might well be sufficient. Indeed, for some people five minutes might be just right and the activity that is going to happen next might provide a natural break or end-point to the session, thus redirecting the person into some other purposeful activity.

Also another issue you might need to keep in mind is: do you need to check any requirement for toileting, or for drinks, or for any other timetable issues before you start?

How long have you got – is it going to be long enough?

When working with a person who is unfamiliar to you

This really depends on your context, what you aim to achieve and what setting you are working in. When you are thinking about working with someone who is unfamiliar, you might not need a long time, as it is entirely likely that because the person doesn't know you, you won't have much to 'chat' about. Interactions build up as a reflection of the relationship you have with someone; so conversations with strangers can tend to be quite short initially, especially so if you cannot find a topic of mutual interest to explore – although this is not always the case.

If time is pressing, it might be beneficial to just watch the person from a distance and confirm your observations. Alternatively you might just approach the person and greet them, then wait for some sort of response or indication of any awareness – you might sit next to them or stand around and just 'be' for a while, to see what develops.

If you have previously done useful observations and you have already considered how you might respond to the person when they're engaged in the activities that you now see in front of you, then go and greet them, responding or gently joining in with their focus. If the person is quite active and they have an item with them which they have a particular attachment to or interest in, then you might get one just like it and begin to play with it in a manner that is similar to the way they interact with their item, that is, *doing something that is recognisable to the person.* Remember don't intrude or take an object off the person – they have probably experienced countless staff taking this thing off them already, and you'll just become another person who does things 'to' rather than 'with' them.

If the person cannot move away from you because of their limited mobility, you might sit next to them or in front of them, again acknowledging and/or responding to their response to you. When you have to leave, tell them before you actually leave – if you are unsure whether your voice or conversation is understood, err on the side of their dignity and assume it is. You might give a signal when you do actually leave – possibly waving and saying 'bye'.

When working with a person who is familiar to you

If you already know the person and have some established interactive routines and repertoires, you might continue with the familiar greeting activity or simply idle away your available minutes in comfortable companionship. This might possibly take the form of something as simple as sharing some proximity, watching the same people pass by, or even falling into the person's breathing pattern as you hold their hand. You might begin to explore a couple of sequences of emerging mutual response that you have visited in previous meetings together, which you know fizzle out fairly quickly, but are always enjoyed by the person.

Either way, it is probably not wise to start a well-loved and particularly energetic activity with the person as you only have a couple of minutes. To start something that you usually allow a good amount of time for and not have time to complete this, will just be a let down.

Finally, if you notice the person is alone, unfocused and bored, and you only have a couple of minutes, you might consider taking them an object you know they like, whether it's a piece of paper, a ball or a leaf. If the person is in a wheelchair you might go over and say 'hello', and spend your free couple of minutes checking that they and their cushions, clothes, etc. seem comfortable. Use this time to greet and chat to them in a manner that encourages their response and gives you a chance to acknowledge them and show a bit of care and attention.

It's a judgement call. You will inevitably make mistakes, and you may occasionally feel awkward because you are leaving, but it is always worth saying a friendly 'hello' to someone who otherwise might be isolated.

Other issues that you may need to consider

Will you have time to record what you do, for example on paper or video? Is it important to do that this time? Unless you have a very convenient video camera or assistant, it probably will not be worth videoing such a short interaction. If you have a convenient camera and setting it up does not intrude on the already brief interaction, well, it might well be worth pressing 'record'... just in case.

It is not imperative to record every fleeting interaction on paper because, as experience shows, your day will become dominated by paper work and you will not be able to sustain it. If something important happens it would be worth making a note of it; for example if the person shows quite clearly that they are upset by you leaving after a very short interaction, you should certainly make a note of that to inform future interactions.

Do you have any necessary resource items available?

When working with a person who is unfamiliar to you

It can be argued that interactions are much more likely to focus on the actual participants if there are no competing elements present. An object can sometimes become a focus for activity in itself, acting to redirect or distract the attention of the person from their potential communication partner (you). It is easy for you to become a victim of the presence of the object, as you may often try to use the object as the basis of the interaction rather than concentrating more closely on the person. Thus, objects can become the 'default' focus of interaction, rather than the connection that emerges from two people exploring each other's responses.

Remember that Intensive Interaction is about communicating – enjoying and exploring the presence of another person, not communicating about a toy, or how to explore it.

Finally, one reason to avoid over-reliance on objects is that their function in the interaction can sometimes become confused, for example the person likes a particular spoon because it shines and is smooth to the touch, but you might wrongly assume that the interest lies in how the person flaps it. Thus, you may use the spoon in a manner which makes no sense to the person. If you are starting out from a position of not knowing what kinds of objects or resource items a person might have particular interest in or attachment to, then it is perhaps best to put ideas of joint-focus activities around sensory or other resource items to one side.

You might also refer to your observations to reacquaint yourself with the person's preferences and, unless your observations provided you with some evidence that the person often positively engages in the exploration or manipulation of objects, it will most often be best to interact with the person on a human level, 'one to one'. Using yourself and your behaviours, and the person themselves and their behaviours as the resources around which to socialise, will almost certainly be the most productive starting point. You, the practitioner, are by far the best, most adaptable and interesting piece of equipment in your workplace.

Even if, from your observations, a person demonstrates a particular attachment to an object or resource item (and quite possibly has something with them when you first meet, e.g. bunches of keys, pieces of material, hand-held mirrors, small musical instruments, even toy animals or cars) it is best to be very sensitive around engaging with the person based on joint attention to, or exploration of, that item as they might simply want to own it.

However, some clients will be happy to share items or activity involving items, and they might even wish to play a game or create a routine around an object or resource item. Sensitivity to the person's body language and their openness to your presence will be needed in order to see exactly what the person wishes to do. For example, do they hold a particular thing very close and/or do they leave the object lying around or casually drop it?

Sometimes joint focus activities around favoured objects or resource items can be an obvious starting point of a period of Intensive Interaction, but you should still be tentative and sensitive. You need to see what your attempts at initially approaching the person bring, in terms of their responses, that is positive, negative, or as yet non-committal.

If you are going to engage with someone successfully, you have to start somewhere, and sometimes a favoured object that the person currently focuses on, or actively engages with, might give you just the starting point. Demonstrably showing interest in or joining in with a person's current behaviour can be the point from which to move forward.

When working with a person who is familiar to you

When you get to know people better you develop a good knowledge of any objects or resource items that they have attachments to, or find particular interest in. Using these objects and the person's associated behaviour with the object as a basis for interactivity might, for some people, be a useful route into interactivity (either giving or sharing attention on the object or the associated activity, or possibly even introducing another similar object, or an object with similar characteristics, into the social exchanges). However, you would need to proceed sensitively, as some people might be wary of your attempts at such joint attention, although for other people it might be a useful starting point.

If someone demonstrates particular attachment to or interest in a type of object, you could look to analyse the characteristics of that object to see if you could introduce a variation. The new object should be sufficiently similar to still gain the person's interest, while perhaps having some additional or varied characteristic. For example, if the person likes to manipulate parts of their clothing, could a separate piece of cloth also take their interest and make Intensive Interaction easier? If a person likes to flick string, beads, or laces, could you introduce different colours and thicknesses of, for example, strings, beads, or laces that you could share attention around? If a person apparently likes to explore or play games with balls, could you gradually introduce a variety of balls with different colours, textures and surface characteristics?

However, you should proceed cautiously with exchanges based on resource items, as true interactivity can often suffer at the expense of enhanced sensory stimulation for the person with the social or communicative impairment. You should in fact be doubly cautious as it might be that your aims for variety are becoming the dominant driver of the interaction. It might in fact be better to look at a more subtle exploration of the same items, for example exploration of a range of rhythmical exchanges that would be more truly participatory and thus genuinely interactive on the person's part.

Other issues that you may need to consider

Depending on where you are working with someone, there may be many or few resource items available. Certainly it is not unusual to have many toys (perhaps too many toys), immediately available if you are working with children in their own homes. This can sometimes be a distraction from any attempt at interactivity, and so it might sometimes be better (if it is all right with the child and the carers) to put the majority of items out of sight before commencing a period of Intensive Interaction. By contrast, in some institutional environments there are very few interesting objects that are freely available for people to explore or engage with.

For some people, particular items might only interest them for a certain period of time before becoming too familiar or even boring, through excessive exposure. In such circumstances alternating or sequencing a person's access to a number of different toys or resource/ sensory items can keep them fresh and avoid any over-familiarity.

Sometimes cleanliness can be an issue with some objects that have a particular interest and attraction for people with a communicative or social impairment. Keeping such items clean, especially if someone explores them with their mouth, can be an issue that needs some thought. Regular cleaning (with warm soapy water) or use of alcohol wipes to clean the surfaces of any such objects, and your hands, might be necessary. Another method is possibly to pass objects through a washing machine or dishwasher on occasions.

<u>CHAPTER 2</u> What to Do and Think About While Using Intensive Interaction

What can you do to engage someone – what techniques can you use?

When working with a person who is unfamiliar to you

As has been said in previous sections, you are trying to find common ground with the person during the early stages of an interactive partnership, so whatever you do should be recognisable to and resonant with the person. If you are recognisable and familiar, you will be understandable to them.

Assuming that you have observed and identified some frequent behaviours, or the person's current focus of interest that you think you can respond to, your first decision is choosing the moment to respond and then how to adjust your initial responses so that they fit into the person's pauses. This style of response highlights the fact that you are responding to the person, and from the person's perspective this makes you controllable.

When trying to socially engage someone who is not yet familiar, imitation or mirroring is often a valuable technique. While some movements or sounds will be easy to imitate or reflect back, it is important to try to identify the 'why' as well as the 'what' of the activity you are responding to. Standing nearby and imitating someone who repeatedly waves a leaf might well gain their attention, but standing nearby imitating them as they grind their teeth will probably be less successful if the person is engaged in this because they enjoy the sensation of their jaw compression or the vibration achieved.

As you want to attract their attention to what you are doing, rather than to the other events that might simultaneously and continually compete for their attention, your initial task is to find a quality of response that intrigues your communication partner while also reflecting their rhythm and arousal level as closely as possible.

A few phrases and names have emerged that describe some of the different strategies that practitioners often use. The following list is certainly not exhaustive or prescribed practice, but it will be useful.

GIVING 'GOOD FACE'

This phrase draws attention to the importance of the skilled communication partner presenting themselves prominently in the person's field of view or awareness. You should ensure that you are physically available – facing the person if appropriate, using exaggerated vocal intonation, and expressive and responsive facial expressions. Most often a slightly to one side or off-centre angle is the best position, as straight or square on face-to-face positioning can feel uncomfortable and even a little threatening at times.

If any touch is used to make the person aware of your presence it should always be carried out within the usually accepted conventions of care (and in accordance with any service or organisational policies) and involve non-intimate areas of the body. It is important that any touch/physical contact is dynamic (e.g. a rhythmical hand squeezing) or constantly moving, as to the skin's sensory receptors stationary physical contact becomes 'dead weight' in very little time.

'Good face' then, relates to the degree of presence that you use to announce your availability.

BURST-PAUSE

This term is often used to describe the process in which communication partners respond to each other in conversation – that is, both partners involved in a dialogue wait until the end of the other's utterance before beginning their own. This is an inherent process in learning about turn-taking and mutual adjustment. Within Intensive Interaction, it is often used to describe the manner in which the skilled partner helps to give structure and rhythm to an interaction by synchronising their contribution to fill the pause left between their partner's pulses of behaviour. The person may simply be repeating a burst of sound or behaviour without particular reference to you or awareness of the interactive potential of the situation; however, you might use this technique to highlight the responsive nature of the emerging dialogue.

Skilful use of a burst-pause strategy can build interest and anticipation for the person in what is to come next, for example by judiciously holding back on an expected response or aspect of behaviour to heighten the game-like or fun aspect of the interaction.

IMITATION

While the person may demonstrate pulses of behaviour which include regular pauses that are convenient to respond to interactively, you might also observe that the person demonstrates long pulses of behaviour with very short, unpredictable pauses (e.g. when the pause lasts long enough for the person to inhale quickly). In the first scenario, it is easy for you to reflect back a response that is very similar or closely linked to the behaviours of the person. Within the second scenario you may be concerned that your response will go largely unnoticed, due to the brevity of the space left between the person's behaviours for you to respond to. In this case, imitation might involve reflecting back or echoing the person's behaviour simultaneously with them. While this may eventually result in gaining the person's attention and subsequently to burst-pause-imitation, it might also eventually lead to an equally responsive game in which the person explores and celebrates the different aspects of mutual adjustment and shared activity.

REFER/ECHO

If a person has a visual or hearing impairment, imitation might be problematic. In such a case you could try responding to the rhythm or timbre of a person's behaviour using a different sensory channel – tap out their vocal rhythm on their arm, hand, or on a nearby table; stroke out their breathing pattern on their arm; squeeze out the rhythm of their jaw clenching on their hand, arm or shoulder. Find out which manner of response attracts the person's attention most and respond in this way, either during the pause or in time with the pulse. (Please note that it may be best to respond to teeth grinding in the pause, as attention is often focused on the sensation or sound of the compressed jaw and teeth.)

Experience indicates that, rather than encouraging the person to persist in these types of behaviour, the person usually notices and orients to the social response they achieve. People frequently demonstrate less of an inclination to immerse themselves in any repetitive or sensory behaviours, as their focus gradually adjusts to the social responses they achieve, rather than to the solitary sensory events they generate, because of boredom, anxiety, or the need for the comfort of repetition.

SLIGHT ADJUSTMENT

While it is certainly a technique that might promote the exploration of new ground when working with someone who is familiar, it might be explored with someone new, following a serial exchange or extended dialogue which has followed a constant theme. By slightly adjusting a contribution from what is expected, such as slightly deviating from a well-developed pattern of clapping hand contacts, you can monitor whether the person appears to show playful interest or raised anxiety. If the response is interest, you might repeatedly and rhythmically revisit the adjustment (possibly adding some drama and playful tension) to investigate whether the person shows signs of anticipation and pleasure. This in turn might lead to a new game or format. However, if the adjustment is met with repeated indifference, or anxiety, you should return to safe repetition.

SMILE/ACKNOWLEDGE

It is important to be happy and to enjoy interactions and it is equally important that the person you are working with is aware that you are enjoying it. The majority of the exchanges that people with intellectual disabilities experience in services relate to functional or needs-based transactions. It is vitally important for all of our emotional wellbeing and sense of self that we learn that we are liked; good to be with; and that being social is good. A nurturing touch or a nod of acknowledgement from across a room is hugely important for the recipient's spirit, especially if they are socially isolated. However, caution should be used not to over-do the direct and occasionally invasive use of touch, facial expression or gaze with someone with whom you are not familiar.

BACK OFF

Be aware that if you are working with someone who is unfamiliar to you, then *you* are unfamiliar to *them*. So the approach of an unfamiliar practitioner may be tainted by previous, possibly unpleasant experiences with staff members more concerned with compliance than empowerment. If your approach appears to raise arousal or anxiety, back off and find the distance with which the person is comfortable – you might imitate or respond noticeably to their behaviours from that distance, or you might simply move slightly into the space, being guarded and *immediately back off if you see the anxiety signs begin to emerge*. You will now be having a conversation about proximity, while at the same time, the person is learning that you will acknowledge them and respond to their behaviour.

When working with a person who is familiar to you

It is always a good idea to discuss the interactive strategies which engage the person with whom you are planning to socialise with someone who knows them or who has already established some interactive routines with them. The list is similar when working with someone who is familiar, although there are some slightly altered aspects of use.

GIVING 'GOOD FACE'

This strategy always applies, except now you might be able to capitalise on your shared recognition and be able to use your availability as an offer to interact – for example, greet from a distance and see if you get an invitation to come closer.

BURST-PAUSE

By now it is hoped that your contribution or responses will have been noticed, and so your 'answer' might have been accommodated into any interactive routine or repertoire. The person might monitor you and respond to your response. It is not to be assumed that this *should* happen, as it depends wholly on the level of intellectual disability or social isolation that the person experiences. It might take minutes, days, weeks or years for the person to recognise that your response relates to their behaviour. If you feel you are not 'getting on the person's intellectual radar', re-visit your observations; spend more time watching them; video your attempts to engage the person and watch for less obvious responses that you might be missing; get the opinion of a trusted and experienced colleague; watch someone else interacting with the person.

Remember, if you continue to use the same solution to a problem, you'll only get the same outcome.

IMITATION

As you get to know a person it is likely that when you reflect on how you interact together you will realise that you have fallen into a pattern of greetings, and have gently established a way of 'being' with the person. You might begin by imitating them or joining in with their focus, or simply by sitting with them and acknowledging their glance.

As you find that these interactive repertoires of response emerge, you might try and vary the way you respond – for example hesitating to 'tease' out a pause, while watching to see if the person tries to hurry you up, or indicate that they were expecting you to fall in with the usual structure of the interaction. You might also explore responses which, while being very similar to what the person offers you, are slightly different, or extended, to see if this variation is taken on board by the person. You should always be watchful to see if the person is trying the same thing out on you too. Remember, it is supposed to be fun – so play with opportunities, be jovial and affirmative, and use dramatic exaggeration and timing.

REFER/ECHO

With familiarity established, echoes might go from one version of the behaviour to another within the same interaction, for example tapping out your response on the person's hand, then on their shoulder, then on your own leg – move it about . A game might emerge where you explore the enjoyment of anticipating where your next response is to be made. You might even vary the speed of the rhythm or volume of the vocal response you make, to see if that engages the person's interest or creates a shared sense of fun.

ANTICIPATION

When the structure of a responsive routine or game has emerged, it may be worthwhile responding playfully to the suggestions of the person. The use of deliberately extended pause, pretend surprise, exaggerated acknowledgement and celebration are key aspects here. You might also try playful sabotage, which is actually a variation on 'anticipation games'.

SABOTAGE

This is the name often given to a nuance in game-playing in which the skilled communication partner might purposefully respond 'incorrectly' within the structure of the game – for example when the person expected you to clap with them, you decide to stomp your foot; or pretend to be distracted; or simply do something 'wrong'. The point of 'sabotage' is three-fold:

- Your action will motivate the person to communicate something.

- Your incorrect action provides the 'content' for the person to comment about.

- By immediately responding to their comment, by rejoining the game, you support them to 'repair' the interaction.

Gentle sabotage gives the person the opportunity to rehearse being a social agent; your immediate response to whatever it is that the person does (in response to the 'problem') provides them with the satisfaction of control, as well as the opportunity to restart and re-establish *their* game.

So while *hesitation* in a game involves the practitioner pausing before following on with their turn, *sabotage* involves them doing something that gently disrupts the flow of the exchange. Sabotage needs to be used carefully, so as not to confuse or disorient the person. Within very established interactive partnerships, this sabotage can often develop into a game in its own right – offering the person the opportunity to change interactive repertoires, default to a more comforting or more established exchange or setting up a point from which to explore something completely different.

SMILE/ACKNOWLEDGE

Understanding and using smiles, nods and confirming touch are some of the fundamental elements of communication. They are also some of the most complex and subtle aspects of being social, and they are clearly very difficult to de-code for many people with autistic spectrum disorders or complex physical and sensory conditions. Experienced Intensive Interaction practitioners come to use carefully exaggerated and extended facial and vocal expressions to expand the sequence and interplay of interactive exchanges within well-established partnerships. Once the person is comfortable with your presence and you are sure that your gaze or dramatic facial expressions are not intrusive, then you can go on to explore interactive repertoires of responsive facial expression.

However, it is important not to get carried away with *your* idea of how the game should proceed. Remember the practitioner's role is to be responsive. While some people delight in the security of their familiar interactive repertoires, others find comfort and security in repetition; you should respect this aspect of how a person can enjoy your presence with them. Nevertheless, there is a clear tension, because it is also part of your role to support the exploration of the communicative potential of social exchanges and to present opportunities for the rehearsal of social agency. These ideas simply introduce degrees of variety into established interactive routines, to help to avoid them continuously falling within unnecessarily limited or 'default' patterns.

Thinking back to your observations – what have you learned, and what should you be looking for now?

When working with a person who is unfamiliar to you

If a person is unfamiliar to you then it is likely that you will not have had much time in which to have made a thorough or extended observation of them, or their current behaviour. This does not mean that you should not be attempting to interact with the person, but it will almost certainly mean that you will be more tentative in your attempts to engage with them, and more acutely observant of any potential responses that they might be making back to you.

It might well be possible that the person has already attempted to initiate some interactivity, and it would be unwise and impolite not to give them some response in acknowledgement of this. However, you should generally be more tentative in your attempts at responding, and so you may respond at a slightly slower tempo, and perhaps even slightly less intensely, introducing yourself socially, while trying not to increase a person's levels of anxiety.

This slower and more tentative introductory tempo may be made apparent through:

- A more cautious exploration of proximity – do not jump into the person's personal space too soon, perhaps allow them to come to you. Try to be low down if you can be (and if it is safe to do so), preferably as low as, or lower than, the person. Avoid standing over people if at all possible.

- Give softer and more sensitive eye contact, that is, avoid staring or using extended eye contact too much, unless there is obvious acceptance and comfort in this area.

- Use quieter and lower intoned vocalisations – keep your vocal echoing calm and reassuring, keep it positive – perhaps with a rising final affirmative intonation that invites, but does not demand a response.

- Keep your physical movements careful and controlled, while still being open and encouraging.

- If physical contact is acceptable and appropriate during an initial interactive session, engage the person with slower and gentler physical contacts – you can always build up tempo and the level of physicality as time goes on.

It is hoped that by reflecting on these issues or considerations you might be able to come to a view on whether your initial period of observation has suggested any potential strategies that you might be able to exploit in your efforts to interact successfully with the person. Is there some obvious activity that you can join in with or reflect back to the person? This could be, for example, physical movements or activity; vocalisations; body sounds or noises made with the mouth; facial expressions; physical contacts or even self-involved or stereotyped behaviour (Nind and Hewett 2001).

It is always important initially to work in a provisional or conditional way, using contemporaneous observations to inform your current presentations (and your future attempts at interaction). So once you have shared any initial period of interactivity, it is again necessary to actively *reflect* on any useful observations you have continued to make:

- How has the person responded to your proximity – should you move nearer, further away or stay put?

- Have they made eye contact? Do they look at you or away when you are near to them, or move nearer?

- Have they initiated any physical contact?

- Have they vocalised in any way, and is there any particular rhythm, tone or pattern to their vocalisations that might have communicative significance?

- Are they more or less vocal when you respond in some way?

- What responses have they given to your social availability and tentative interactivity?

- Do they move or turn away from you when you are near to them, or move nearer?

- Does their facial expression change when you respond in some way?

- Do they seem more or less anxious with you near them, or do they seem intrigued by or indifferent to your proximity or behaviour? How do they show this?

- Does the tempo of their activity, or even their breathing pattern, increase or decrease as you attempt to interact with them?

- Does their pallor or muscle tone change as you attempt to interact, and if so how?

- Does the person's activity change in any observable way (e.g. in its form or tempo) when your attention is on them, or does it cease altogether?

Answering the following questions will help to avoid overextending any initial period of interaction:

- Does any initial eye contact feel rather harsh or has it an overly staring quality?

- Should you look away for a short while and see what the person does?

- Are your vocal responses over-arousing the person?

- Should you quieten to a whisper and see what the person does?

- The person's attention seems to have waned – should you move away, or just pause for a while and see what the person does, that is, do they need a short rest rather complete termination of the session?

As you get to know a person better you will be able to answer such questions more easily and more certainly, and then any Intensive Interaction will be much better informed and will almost certainly flow more naturally (Nind 1996).

When working with a person who is familiar to you

As familiarity comes you will know what signals to look for and be more confident in your interpretations of the feedback you get from the person. It is hoped that you will have built a rapport and also a repertoire of different Intensive Interaction routines that you can both recognise, participate in and mutually take pleasure from. However, you should never take previous successes for granted, and you will need to continue to be keenly observant of a person's feedback to your presence and interactivity. All the questions and issues noted above will still be pertinent as you look to build on, and, it is hoped, develop, subtle variations on the routines and interactive games that have developed between you already.

When working with people with whom you are familiar, you might look at their initial responsiveness, hoping to be reassured that you are still getting things right for them. You might also wish to match your particular Intensive Interaction routine to the current environment in which you find yourselves. All the things you can do to help the person to sustain their attention on any potential interactivity should be considered.

If you know the person well you might decide that the place where you find yourselves is potentially distracting or uncomfortable for them, and so you may wish to think about moving somewhere better. Perhaps you might need to arrange the room you are in to suit the person better, or even move them out of a chair (do you need a hoist?) or into a particular preferable or favoured position (if the person has particular favoured places or positions perhaps you might have to sit on bean-bags, or on a settee, or in individual chairs at 90° to each other).

Another question to usefully ask yourself might be:

- Can you change the sound environment to one that is more suited to the person you are working with? Perhaps you should put on some low-level ambient music to block out any distracting noises from outside?

Also you might ask yourself:

- Is the lighting all right (sometimes halogen or strip lighting can be too harsh and can even upset some people who are hypersensitive to this – i.e. some people with autism)? Do you need to take some action here?

Other issues that you may need to consider

It may be necessary to consider the more general environmental issues that might affect the chances of successfully engaging people in Intensive Interaction:

- Are there other distractions in the room that might need to be addressed or removed?

- Are there other people in the room that might need attending to, or who may in some way affect the intensity or sustainability of your intended Intensive Interaction?

Potential distractions that might affect or deflect the attention of either person should be addressed ideally as early as possible, although generally Intensive Interaction can happen anywhere, anytime, anyplace, and it is sometimes all right, or mostly even preferable to just go with the flow.

How do you know if the person is ready for Intensive Interaction?

When working with a person who is unfamiliar to you

The most important thing to do before you approach someone, whether they are familiar or not, is to watch them for a couple of moments. You are looking for an 'alert-relaxed' state. What this looks like will be different for everyone, which is why you will have done some observations and will be able to compare how the person is now with how you have seen them before. Periods of anxiety, agitation, distress or exhaustion are probably not the best time to try out early interactions.

If they seem relaxed and alert, you should approach and greet the person, being careful not to crowd them or invade their space too rapidly (as discussed previously) and interact with them in the manner you had considered beforehand – imitating, joining in, pulsing in similar rhythms or simply being near and acknowledging their activity.

If the person seems completely immersed in their chosen activity, you might watch whether their tempo or pace increases as you get closer – is their activity a defensive reaction helping them to displace their anxiety at some aspect of your presence? Does it calm as you withdraw?

There can come a point in some interactions when a practitioner begins to wonder whether the person is aware of them or not. This is usually brought on by their impression that they are not being responded to or monitored. At this early stage this is not important, because *you* are there to respond, not them. They might be aware of you, but at this stage might not recognise your social availability. In these early stages, the person quite possibly isn't sure of *how* to engage you, or s/he has already tried but you didn't recognise their invitation. Now might be a good time to begin videoing the interactions to check to see if you are missing something.

In the early stages of an interactive partnership, what you are trying to achieve is to *intrigue* the person and draw their attention on to you. If your interactive attempts are not responded to, then you may need to re-look at your observations again for another strategy. If you have a fallback plan, then use it; for example, try a couple of the different manners of responding to their behaviour, before leaving.

As a rule of thumb though, if you are sure that the interaction is not going to happen, try making a 'feint' or obvious signal of imminent departure. If your apparent leaving achieves a brief capture of their attention, then they were aware of you. So maybe next time, a repeated 'feint to leave' could become part of an emerging game of shared anticipation.

Even within interactions that seem to be going really well, it is also important to monitor the person for signs of tension, body language or postural changes that are beginning to be more defensive, or possibly any increasing excitement. Sometimes for some people great amusement or happiness can well up into over-arousal, leading to a level of unmanageable excitement – so you should be wary of allowing an interaction to develop in such a manner. If spiralling excitement is a repeated feature of interactions then you need to identify the types of interactivity that cause such excitement, so that you can consider how to support the person to encounter it more constructively and with greater emotional equilibrium, for example by doing something slowly and more quietly, and possibly over a shorter period.

When working with a person who is familiar to you

The means here are similar to the above, although you should have more knowledge about what anxiety, distress, pleasure and over-excitement might look like. If you are going to work with the person, spend a couple of minutes waiting to see their mood and decide whether, based on your experience with them, it is a good time for them, and they are likely to be interested in you. If you are planning to work with them in the near future consider whether there are particular times or places when your offer of interaction has worked well before – is there a pattern? Can you positively exploit such a pattern?

As you approach, do they glance at you; smile to themselves/ at you; turn toward you; invite you? Do they become still? Use your inbuilt capacity to read the situation just as you would before beginning an exchange with a colleague or acquaintance. Remember to watch continually throughout the interaction for patterns of response or signs that you are being too intrusive. If the person moves away from you, don't terminate and give up immediately, but hang around looking interested and they might well return.

Is this the best time to try and start – does it have to be now?

There may be a number of issues that inform your decision making about exactly when it is the best time to start your Intensive Interaction. This might be very similar for people who are both familiar and unfamiliar to you, and you can only go on what you currently know about the person concerned and the situation as you perceive it. As stated previously, a good rule to follow is one that employs a tenet of *sensitive optimism*, that is, that now is generally the best time to start any Intensive Interaction, unless there are clear, observable and valid reasons to the contrary, that is, with respect to the person, the environment and yourself as a practitioner.

So, in practice you would generally proceed with a view that *now* is *all right* to start your attempt at Intensive Interaction unless you know of a good reason not to start, or you know that a better time to interact is likely to come along in the near future.

The main reason that you may not proceed with initiating an interaction is if it is not acceptable to the person with a communicative or social impairment. Sometimes people are, for a variety of reasons, just not in the right mood to accept your initiations. This could be due to the time of day (it might be too early or too late) or to the person not feeling 100% in terms of their health or general wellbeing (possibly due to recent, current or looming epileptic activity), or they might be physically uncomfortable, hungry or thirsty, or there may even be a reason that you cannot know about and may remain hidden to you.

However, such personal issues might not be sufficient reason not to engage in an interaction, and you may think about modifying the tempo or the types of strategies that you use to engage the person instead: try to be aware of whether you are looking for reasons not to interact, and if you are, reflect on why this might be, and perhaps discuss with a confidant or colleague.

Your perceptions about the suitability or safety of the immediate environment (and any other people in the environment) might influence your decision about whether to begin an interaction. Questions you might reflect on include:

- Is the environment too chaotic or distracting?

- Are you too physically uncomfortable or cramped?

- Are there too many people around requiring some level of attention, making it difficult for either of you to focus on interacting in a relaxed and focused manner?

- Is something or some other potential activity visibly distracting, for example a full teapot or tray of biscuits?

Remember: you could think about moving somewhere less distracting or moving any distractions out of sight or out of the way!

Other issues worthy of consideration might include your own potential for distraction and whether you might unavoidably be called on to undertake or attend to some other task in the near future which could mean that you might not have the necessary time to engage sensitively. You would not want to withdraw suddenly from the interactive session and leave your partner 'hanging on', or waiting for a response that doesn't come.

Potentially there might be issues related to time; you could ask yourself if there might be more chance of interacting more successfully and over a more sustained period at another time in the near future.

However, in most circumstances that you and your clients or learners are likely to find yourselves in, you should not generally encounter many issues that genuinely disallow Intensive Interaction, and so it should usually be a good time to at least attempt some form of Intensive Interaction.

Other issues that you may need to consider

While it is always best to be able to formalise some ring-fenced time for interaction, it is also very important to take advantage of less formal opportunities. If you use an opportunistic approach to Intensive Interaction, then you should be actively looking for regular opportunities throughout the day to start periods of Intensive Interaction. Interactions can run alongside or be simultaneous with other activities, for example during hydrotherapy, massage or personal care tasks. Using such an opportunistic approach, you are more likely to find the times when the person is in the right mood to be receptive although sometimes, inevitably, you may find that this occurs when the environment and staffing levels are not ideal.

However, such opportunistic types of working invariably lead to the situation where no one feels fully responsible for engaging the person interactively, and eventually at the end of a day no one has actually gone ahead and done so. Thorough recording strategies are required so that the potential for such lapses are minimised.

The best approach to providing Intensive Interaction is, in our view, an amalgamation of both approaches, with some structure in terms of overt timetabling of Intensive Interaction and staff involved, combined with an opportunistic approach. This ensures that when the best times for Intensive Interaction present themselves, and the person is potentially at their most receptive; carers and staff have the flexibility to 'go with the flow' and engage sociably with them.

How do you approach the person – what do you do first?

When working with a person who is unfamiliar to you

How you approach someone will be influenced by context and environmental issues: as mentioned earlier you will have to think about what is going on in the room you are working in – are there a lot of distracting and/or unpredictable noises or distractions?

If the person you are working with has a hearing loss or you have noticed them startling, or if they seem to be sensitive to loud noises, it may be best (at least initially) to find a time or place where these distractions are diminished.

It is important that interactions are not seen as something you do in a quiet side-room, or that require special settings. However, it is equally important that if the person has difficulty separating your presence from the competing events going on nearby, at least in the early stages of your interactions, you might consider finding somewhere more predictable or calm to introduce the idea of interaction and mutual response. Clearly, this will depend on whether there is somewhere else to go.

In unpredictable environments, the use of touch (if welcomed and responded to) can become even more important to maintain focus and contact, as it can sooth and create a constant link between partners. If you are inescapably in a noise-filled room, it may be advantageous to respond to the qualities of the movement, facial expression or physical touch that you observe in the person's repertoire, to begin your exploration of social responding from these points.

Using your observations and your knowledge of the person you are approaching gain their attention using your eyes, smile, open body posture, or imitation to announce your availability. If the person is in a wheelchair, be sure to present yourself at the right height, preferably at or below the person's eye level (a note of caution here – be careful not to bend your back as this can, if overdone, lead to wear and tear and potential damage to your spine – sit on a chair or stool, crouch down by bending your knees, or even sit or kneel on the floor).

If your communication partner has a visual impairment or no sight, it is important that you do not become yet another experience that invades their awareness, so prepare them before you initiate touch, using a 'sensory signature'.

If you are certain that the person can discriminate your presence, the best thing to do might be nothing – that is, to 'hover' nearby and see if you are approached. If you do decide to approach the person, do so gradually and apparently nonchalantly, remembering to let the person decide the final distance between you.

When working with a person who is familiar to you

You should now have more knowledge about how best to approach the person and crucially they will have more experience of what sort of things you get up to together. How you approach still depends on context and environmental issues.

Your options are:

- to approach until you feel your presence is acknowledged or welcomed then wait for the person to suggest a game activity/greeting/conversation

- to approach when you see your partner focus on an activity that has been the basis of previous successful interactions

- to approach until you feel your presence is acknowledged or welcomed, then suggest a game/activity/greeting/ conversation based on previous successes

- to hover nearby while orienting to the person and wait to be approached or just to see what happens, or

- to find somewhere where you are sure the person can see/sense you and begin to move/vocalise/act using the idiosyncrasies you have regularly observed to be 'of' them, and see if they approach and join you.

Alternatively, it may be useful to develop some predictability – for example, over previous interactions a sequence of mutual acknowledgement or response may have emerged, or you may have 'happened on' a mutually recognised 'greeting' (e.g. intense eye contact, a pattern of vocalisations, movements or physical contacts, even saying hello). This may have emerged in previous interactions through your responses to the person or their response to you, becoming a mutually recognised signal that they are happy to see you and engage with you. If the person has a favourite object, bring your own (rather than sharing theirs) to announce your interest in their focus.

Always be conscious not to hurry things along. Don't be too quick to jump into a pause with imitation or 'your' idea of what should happen next. Remember, when the person pauses in their activity, it might be that they are watching whether you will pause too, or indeed they might just be resting. Explore and adapt to the cadence of activity from your partner and watch for their approval or consent about your response – this may be periodic and you may well realise that you have misread a cue. Do not worry unduly if this happens occasionally; interactions are not brittle or irreparable, and it is the person's familiarity with the structure of encounters which emerges with repetition over time, which form the mutually recognisable routines and games.

What should you be looking for as you go along?
When working with a person who is unfamiliar to you

As you respond to the person, the question you might be asking yourself is *what is the point of what they're doing as far as they're concerned?'... Is the behaviour intentionally communicative, that is, directed at you, or is it indicative?* Does the behaviour carry information about what it's like to 'be' that person at the moment? You could also think about whether you have seen this sort of activity before, that is, in previous interactions, and if so, in what context? Reflecting on these issues should help to provide some tentative insight into the potential feelings and perceptions of the person you are working with or caring for.

When you watch other people, you make inferences about their internal emotional 'state' fairly intuitively, by observing how they carry themselves, their expressions, their posture, their activity. These aspects of a person's behaviour can be unintentionally communicative. Some people may never actually communicate purposefully, whether because the profound degree of their intellectual disability has compromised their learning about the effects that their behaviours have on those around them, or disrupted their acquiring an understanding of social cause and effect.

These people may therefore be unaware of the communicative nature of their actions and the actions of those around them. By watching a person's responses to experiences which they encounter, for example pleasure, displeasure or curiosity, one can often infer meaning, even when the person had no *intention* to communicate anything. In books and articles about intellectual disability this type of communication is often referred to as *pre-intentional communication*.

Always be mindful that the way in which a person is behaving might be linked to a range of influences, including any events that occurred before you arrived.

It is important to remember that the way you express emotions has been culturally shaped by social conventions and customs. The person you are working with is unlikely to be aware of such social conventions and customs, and so pleasure or anxiety may well be expressed by them without inhibition, or it may be expressed in a manner at odds with the way you might usually recognise. Also, the actions and focuses of activity you see from the person may well confuse you or seem banal, but they may be very pleasurable for the person who is involved in them. Your observations and reflections are crucially important to enable you to recognise the idiosyncrasies of the person, as is any information you might be able to get from people who have known him/her for longer than you have.

If you think that a behaviour is directed at you, the chances are that you noticed a pause, a glance or some exchange that signalled that you were the target or that the person was watching to see your response. When working with a person who is unfamiliar respond by acknowledging, imitating or affirming it. At this very early stage in your relationship, your main interest is in forging some responsive connection with the person.

Clearly, if you think that the function of the behaviour relates to issues of immediate physical discomfort, try to identify what is wrong; for example, find out how long the person has been sitting in one position in their wheelchair, or try to ascertain whether their mouth is dry, etc. Look for physical needs that may need addressing, for example incontinence pads, muscle cramp, etc.

Proceeding further

Having ensured that the person is comfortable and at a relaxed/alert level of arousal, look for something in their behaviour that you can join in with. *What is their focus of attention?*

You should have already considered how you might join in with the person, or get an invitation to do so, as you reflected on your initial observations. If the behaviours you are seeing now are different, it may not be the best time to intrude or announce yourself. However, as you observe, note whether there are pauses in their activity, and perhaps whether you can position yourself so that they will notice you when you begin to demonstrate the same behaviours if and when they pause. Do you notice the person stilling, orienting more in your direction, or smiling?

It could be that they have noticed you, and your actions have intrigued them into confirming that what you are doing somehow relates to them. Of course if they move away, it might be that you have got too close too quickly, or did too much too closely, or indeed too little, too far away to be noticed.

Assuming they haven't moved off, watch for the focus of their attention and try to identify what the function of the behaviour might be – are they generating pleasure through making sounds, through tactile sensation, movement, or by generating sensations by breath holding, hyperventilating or moving repetitively? Can you refer these qualities back to them using qualities of touch, rhythm, posture, or timbre?

It is hoped that you will find that you are falling into a reciprocal encounter where you are able to respond in the person's pauses, and they respond to your contribution with increasing familiarity or expectation. Alternatively, you might be joining in with the person so that you are both involved in the same activity simultaneously, but socially.

When working with a person who is either familiar or unfamiliar to you

When working with someone who is unfamiliar, the skilled communication partner's job is to be responsive, consistent, predictable and intriguing. As you meet subsequently, you might try to revisit repertoires of movement, sound, or touch from previous encounters, so that they become 'playfully ritualised' or familiar and recognisable ground for the person. Indeed, they might try out features from previous dialogues, to check if they still work. When this happens it is incredibly important to go with the person's lead, rather than requiring that your perspective of an emerging game or routine is followed.

No matter who you are working with, whether the person is familiar to you or not, you should be looking for the same things as you engage them with Intensive Interaction. Because Intensive Interaction requires high levels of sustained responsiveness and sensitivity in its application, you should be constantly checking on the feedback you are receiving from the person you are working with. You should be looking for a number of things that might be indicative of the person's levels of engagement (e.g. the focus of their attention – is it on you or not) or disengagement (e.g. through boredom with your performance), or for any early signs of anxiety, or that the person's arousal levels might be climbing to a point that they might find difficult to control. Such issues might be evidenced in subtle changes, such as in their breathing patterns (especially if their breathing becomes short with an increasing tempo) or the pace of, or force behind particular physical behaviours (e.g. the speed of someone's pacing, or the force that someone puts into tapping/clapping onto your hands with theirs). Sometimes over-arousal can be demonstrated in a person's excessive intensity of focus on a particular behaviour, to the point that they may become challenging if attempts are made to move on from a particular interactive sequence.

You should constantly be observant of the person's focus of their attention, and whether it is more often and more intensely moving toward you, and whether this is more or less often. This will give you evidence of the kinds of Intensive Interaction strategies that are more or less successful at attracting and holding the person's attention. You should be careful at times not to be overly complex in your use of the Intensive Interaction strategies, and it is sometimes a good idea to resort to simple and singular responses (i.e. ones that are not multi-faceted) so that you can garner clearer evidence of which of the strategies are the most successful. This might mean that you keep quiet when you mirror someone's body movements, or equally keep still when vocally echoing someone's pre-verbal vocalisations. You might just use exchanges of eye contacts and facial expressions, and keep there for quite a while (if that strategy works effectively), or you might just continue to repeat a pattern of gentle physical contacts to someone's hands, arms or legs.

As you proceed you may also be looking for small or potentially hidden behaviours that might indicate some type of potential interactivity (e.g. thumb squeezing or rubbing), that you had not previously observed. As you get to know people your observations of their behaviour should become much more acute, and you might well see patterns of behaviour or a particular focus for their interest that was previously hidden to you. This may have been because either you could not see or hear it, or because you simply did not become aware of it, for whatever reason. Once you get more closely involved with people you tend to become more closely attuned with them and therefore, more aspects of their behaviour or changes in behaviour (e.g. its tempo or slight variations in its format) can become more easily apparent. As change is a possible indicator of social and developmental progression, you should view any changes of format or tempo as a potentially positive move, and something that starts, or continues a progression up an 'interactive spiral' (Nind and Powell 2000) of increasing communicative and interactive sophistication.

As time goes by and you become increasingly mutually familiar, you should be actively on the look out for variation on previous interactive themes, so that you can join in with or reflect back to the person. Equally, you could tentatively offer the person your own variation on any known successful theme. Be sure that your variation is something that is sufficiently recognisable to be reassuringly familiar and thus acceptable, but sufficiently different to be challenging or intriguing. When you do offer your own interactive variations you should resist the temptation to push ahead too quickly for the person just because you want to force progression forward to achieve your own personal or professional goals. But trying to work out what is different-but-not-too-different is a bit of a trial and error process, so don't worry if you get it a bit wrong, you can quickly revert back to the original routine.

As you begin to suggest variations in the forms of interaction games and routines used with a person you can explore their responses to changes in your response times, or in your use of dramatic but well-timed pauses, or even variously timed and relatively undramatic pauses. You can attempt to build periods of purposely staged anticipation within well-rehearsed interactive sequences, deliberately holding back expected responses or aspects of behaviour. You could then look at the person's responses to this type of 'teasing' to see if it might be introduced to build a game-like aspect into previously well-rehearsed and oft-repeated interactive sequences.

It should be remembered that a cardinal rule of Intensive Interaction is to gain and hold the attention of the person with a communicative or social impairment (without recourse to controlling or directive communication means). The aim is then to extend the intensity and time over which you successfully engage in affirmative interaction. You are really interested in evidence of this process actually happening, as well as in what it is that is making this happen for you both.

However, while looking for successful Intensive Interaction strategies, you should, at a more basic level, also be observant of any signs of physical discomfort, or possible fatigue on the part of the person you are working with. Intensive Interaction should never become onerous for either party. You should also keep in mind the particular physical needs that the person might need to be attended to; for example someone's pads might need changing, or their mouth might need wiping, and these issues should never be ignored. No matter how well an interaction is going you should always maintain a person's dignity.

It might also be useful at some point to reflect on what the person might be 'thinking' (or feeling or affectively responding) about interaction. Sometimes an attempt to speculate about the other person's perspective can be useful and can help you to manage a session in a more productive way. You may try to identify 'the point' of the Intensive Interaction from the other person's perspective:

- Do they seem to be fascinated or intrigued by a particular aspect of the Intensive Interaction?

- Do they seem utterly absorbed or even possibly obsessed by a particular aspect of the Intensive Interaction?

- Do they just seem to be relaxed and happy to keep a particular aspect of the Intensive Interaction going?

- Can you deduce anything about your use of Intensive Interaction with them from this?

- Would it be better to continue with or possibly move on from certain strategy with this person?

These are questions you should be regularly asking yourself as you proceed with your Intensive Interaction.

If you are working with someone familiar to you, you will probably have a range of games and interactive routines that you can move between and alternate. This is very useful as it gives you a range of options when you begin to realise that the interaction is becoming over-stimulating or dull. When you decide to offer an alternative is a judgement call and you need to think on your feet to decide which strategy might best be used next, as well as how and when to move on to it from the current activity.

Deliberately using a range of different Intensive Interaction strategies has certain advantages as it can keep a sense of momentum going during a session, often extending the lifetime of certain interactive sequences. It can be a way of finding (or stumbling across) greater variations and combinations of interactive routines than might previously have been apparent. Remember though, as ever, that you should never impose a deliberate range of strategies on someone to fulfil your own objectives. Strategies or 'game-plans' should only be applied for the right interactive reasons (e.g. avoiding over-excitement), and should only be continued with if the person's feedback is positive.

Do you always have to follow the other person's lead, or are there times when you can lead the activity in some way?

This is one of the most asked questions encountered from people at all levels of experience of practice and maybe it can best be answered using yet another analogy from your day-to-day interactions with work colleagues or friends. Just to be certain of what we are discussing, this section does not address changing the lead in terms of changing a topic of conversation, but taking the lead in terms of *who goes first?*

When working with a person who is unfamiliar to you

It is always best to observe, even briefly, the person you are going to work with, from a distance for a couple of minutes especially if they are unfamiliar. Doing so will give you some idea of how anxious they are, or what their interest at that time seems to be, or how they relate to people nearby, etc. This is so that if they stop their activity as you approach, you always have a potential and 'live' topic to suggest as the basis of your greeting. You would not simply burst in on a complete stranger and strike up a conversation about something you are interested in, so you would not do it with someone with an intellectual disability either. However, briefly watching them as they focus on their interest might give you the insight to be able to introduce yourself with the equivalent of something like, 'Hi – I've been told you're interested in paper folding.' Intensive Interaction is about creating common ground. Be constantly watchful of your communication partner's expression and movements indicating any anxiety, distress or preferably interest.

Always be mindful that the prevailing experience that many people with intellectual disability acquire is that unfamiliar people approaching them often means that something unfamiliar and sometimes unwanted is about to happen. Trust, which can sometimes take a long time to develop, is built through familiarity and recognition of common experiences, so always approach someone who is unfamiliar, gently and with sensitivity.

It is of course perfectly acceptable and very desirable that staff members should initiate interactions and conversations. However, using Intensive Interaction, you should only do so if the conversation you initiate is already familiar for the person, that is, it is part of their existing repertoire, especially if they are unfamiliar with you – so observe them carefully and think before you act!

When working with a person who is familiar to you

When working with a person who is familiar to you, you will have much more of an idea about the interactive routines the person enjoys, the things that fascinate them, and the range of their own behaviours that they can perceive or recognise. You will know whether this is a particularly favoured song, or the sound they make as they breathe and move their tongue in their mouth. You can announce your presence or suggest a conversation based on any of the idiosyncrasies of that person you have regularly encountered.

Your memory will be assisted by reflective records of interactions you have already had with this familiar person. These records will detail the repertoires, successful elements or intriguing foci that have been discovered or explored over previous interactions. These previous conversations might be suggested as a familiar way to begin a chat, or as topics you might revisit if a chat stalls or fizzles out.

So it is all right to suggest an *already established* topic of conversation, as long as you don't insist that that is the only option for interaction available, that is, if the person shows no interest, try something else or take the hint that they might want to be alone for a while.

Have you achieved what you hoped for so far – what responses have you had, and were these what you were expecting or not?

When working with a person who is unfamiliar to you

If you ask yourself the question, '*Have I achieved what I hoped for?*' that will very much depend on exactly what it is that you hope for, or what you expect before you start. Extended experiences of many different scenarios of Intensive Interaction with many different people with a range of different impairments and communicative abilities, will eventually give you more of an idea of what to expect. But whenever you work with someone who is unfamiliar to you, it is obviously quite hard to have any well-informed expectations of what can realistically be achieved within an interaction. In such circumstances it is probably best to have quite vague and curtailed expectations of what will happen, and then anything positive that does really happen will at least match and will in all probability exceed those initial expectations. This is almost certainly preferable to being over-confident and setting too high a level of expectation for yourself and your communication partner to match. If your expectations are too high then you are likely to be disappointed or create a perception that a session has failed, when in fact the interaction might have gone as well as possible under the given conditions.

It can at times be worth taking a small break during an interactive exchange to briefly reflect on any positive attainments that have so far accrued (and even passivity might be seen as a positive, if it isn't an outright rejection of your social availability). During such a brief reflective interlude you might reflect on what you have achieved, and what you haven't yet achieved, and you might also consider what you think may happen next.

You should also think about the possible significance of what has just happened, and its possible influence on what might happen at some point further on. Your reflection might focus on how to influence your partner's levels of arousal (if that is a potential issue), or you might consider your positioning, or the pace or tempo of the interactivity, or changing the possible strategies, or even watch for an opportunity to take a short rest, so that both partners have a chance to reflect for a while before progressing with the exchange. If you've been doing it with other people around who know the person, get their feedback.

In a general sense, your expectations should therefore remain flexible as an interaction progresses, and you should continue to be reflective about what might happen next, or later, based on what has happened previously or what is currently happening – there is no set formula and no set pattern to a period of interaction. Remaining keenly observant of any feedback you might be getting, and using your observations and reflections on the responses you are receiving should help inform your current responsiveness and levels of expectation.

When looking to make sense of what has been achieved, your evaluation should not be judged on the basis of individual attainment (or lack of attainment) on the part of the person. It is important to remember that it is the level of *joint* engagement and participation that is the defining issue in the realisation of Intensive Interaction, that is, the quality of the mutual interactivity that is important, rather than individual or specific actions (or inactivity).

When working with a person who is familiar to you

When working with someone you have previously worked with, you are much more likely to have some idea about what to expect during an interactive social exchange. You should be familiar with a range of established interactive routines that have previously worked well with the person. You might know how long someone likes to interact for, and how best to present yourself initially to start an interactive session. You might also know when and where you should start to give yourself the best chance of supporting a successful session. However, you should still remain flexible in your expectations; different sessions will almost inevitably progress in subtly or even completely different ways from previous sessions. You will still need to be reflective 'in the moment' and keenly observant of the person's feedback as a session progresses.

You should not take the person and their previous choices of favoured interactive means for granted. Preferred means of interaction can and do sometimes differ, move on and often develop in terms of their range and levels of sophistication. It might also be possible that previously successful strategies and routines may need some refinement, or may just not be 'the required thing' today (although as a general rule repetition is the structure that supports future development).

What had previously seemed to have been guaranteed favourite activities or routines, inevitable change – subtle shifts in mood or preference may affect the reception of a well-rehearsed routine across different occasions. If you rely on established routines too much and engage in them for too long, they may become restrictive, so you may need to think about how often and over what period you might use a 'favourite' interactive strategy or routine. Sometimes you might have to restrain your need for confirmatory feedback and reflect on how to proceed for best effect in the longer term.

Other issues that you may need to consider

Unexpected occurrences can sometimes be the starting points of a new or an expanded range of interactive means, and so unexpected responses from the person are often the very thing that you would wish for. However, there is never any rush to elicit new responses, which should develop naturally and never be forced. You can, on occasions, invite novel responses by using 'sabotage' – occasionally and subtly altering your own responses to see what the person does in return. Such sabotage, or even 'teasing' (i.e. holding back a response in such a way that promotes the fun or jovial aspect of an interactive sequence), can sometimes seed some unexpected responses. But this should not be done systematically or simply to create novel or unexpected responses – it is great if new responses do occur, but if the person does not respond comfortably, you should quickly revert back to the recognisable and secure routine practised previously.

Are you still being sufficiently observant of the person?

When working with a person who is unfamiliar to you

You will probably only begin thinking this if the person responds to your social advances by walking off, falling asleep or remaining disinterested in, or oblivious to your presence. When any of these things happen consistently, it might be time to:

1. Spend more time observing the person, their behaviour and their interests, and consider how you might respond to the person in a manner that might intrigue or interest them more.

2. Video your interactions and reflect on your responses: are you responding too quickly, too closely, too enthusiastically, or alternatively, do you need to respond with more enthusiasm, or touch? Are you responding in a manner that the person can perceive? Is what you are responding to the real focus of the person's interest?

3. Get someone else to help: don't feel that you are alone in this; openly and honestly discuss such issues or difficulties with colleagues who know the person.

Finally, it might be that the person walks away from you to see if you'll follow, or that they seem disinterested in you…but actually they are still watching you and aren't yet relaxed enough with your presence to engage you or respond without suspicion. It is valuable to remember that many of the people for whom this approach will be used, have great difficulty separating 'staff' from 'friends'. Clients and students who repeatedly experience a high rate of turnover in their 'friends' may be more cautious or not ready to invest in people who regularly 'disappear'.

It may also be worth asking about any other things that might be affecting the person, for example any medication changes (sedation);

any disturbed sleep patterns; or possibly any unwelcome experiences that might lead the person to switch off from other people.

When working with a person who is familiar to you

If you are asking yourself this question in an established relationship, the same applies really. Ask yourself *why* you are wondering this – that is, what is it in the person's behaviour that leads you to think that you are not being observant enough. When in doubt, do more observation before, during and after an interaction. To do this to best effect you will need to structure your observations, and ideally use video.

This particular activity has been going on for quite a long time – should you change what you are doing or just keep going?

When working with a person who is unfamiliar to you

When you are first working with someone and trying to find the initial basis of a successful and sustainable interactive exchange, finding something that works well (e.g. a pattern of reciprocal vocal exchanges or mirroring a pattern of body movement) is the first point to be reached. Once such a pattern is established and mutually accepted, then from that point onwards recognisable repetition of that familiar pattern or vocalisation is often the most certain way of establishing and deepening a connection with that person. So in the early periods of exploring Intensive Interaction with someone, the very fact that a sequence continues to be successful over an extended period of time is something to be aimed towards and celebrated, rather than being viewed negatively as static or unnecessarily duplicated.

It can sometimes be postulated that some people become bored of a particular interactive sequence or routine, and some practitioners have voiced anxieties about becoming over-reliant on certain 'favourite' activities, fearing that the activity might lose its power through becoming overfamiliar. This is not something you should worry too much about, and certainly not in the initial stages of working interactively with someone with a social or communicative impairment. It is almost always 'us' (i.e. carers and staff members) that find repetition the most challenging, and while the same activity continues to motivate a person well enough for them to keep coming back for more, it is generally a sensible approach to go along with this desire, especially in the early stages, when trust and relationship building are at a premium. Remember – you can only move forward at the person's pace, and only when they are ready to proceed!

When working with a person who is familiar to you

When you work repeatedly with people who are familiar, then repetition will always remain the basis from which to proceed forward. However, and this is quite a big 'however', as you continue to develop and repeat a favoured routine or sequence, you might occasionally and tentatively offer the person some subtle 'variations on a theme' of the favoured and familiar routine. If any subtle variation is acknowledged and positively responded to, then you could proceed and possibly even incorporate the variation into building a new conversation. If a variation is not acknowledged or positively responded to, you can always revert back to the previous familiar pattern. Any conversation can occasionally and quite naturally meander off onto a variety of other related topics, but most often they return to issues concerning a single shared interest. So an interactive episode can also sometimes naturally meander, although this should not be overly aimed towards or driven forward by the practitioner. The reassurance of familiarity should not be threatened or jeopardised by your wish for novel variation or observable development towards some externally set developmental 'benchmark' or attainment target.

Use your intuition to recognise when to introduce the 'variations on a theme' previously mentioned. Sometimes within interactive sessions there might be moments when something 'same but different' might be offered to good effect. As stated above though, the pace of any such change should not be forced, and returning to the familiar and recognisable is almost always a good idea at some point. To labour a point – you can only move forward at the person's pace, and only when they are ready to proceed.

Other issues that you may need to consider

Although this is thankfully quite rare, one potential consideration that might indicate against continuous or extended repetition of a favoured activity is if there are any early indications that prolonged repetition might potentially develop into challenging behaviour due to a person's spiralling arousal levels. Such a situation is, however, usually avoidable by keeping the activity quite short, or by controlling, or periodically reducing the activity's tempo or vigour.

Sometimes it is preferable, and even explicitly advisable, to sequence short periods of higher tempo intensive interactivity with periods of reduced interactivity across a period of time for some people who can exhibit challenging behaviour. This can help sustain their engagement without over-challenging their capacity to regulate their own calmness or composure.

What are you hoping to achieve in the whole session?

When working with a person who is unfamiliar to you

At this point, you are hoping to get on the person's 'intellectual radar' for a pleasantly memorable meeting. You are hoping to engage the person in a social exchange in which they find pleasure and comfort in the company of another human being. You are hoping to establish a level of acknowledgement, involvement or interest that can be revisited next time you meet. You are hoping that you will notice the features of your responses that the person likes most or shows most interest in.

As your early interactions progress, you are trying to build up a familiar pattern of interactivity and you should be watching for patterns in the way the person responds or acts. The patterns might be to do with the person's gaze or the way s/he might try to explore you through touch; their behavioural idiosyncrasies and rhythms of activity; their responses; the precursors to changes of interactive repertoires; or the way that offers of transactions are made. During the early interactions it is important to be ready to change topics of conversation in response to changes in the person's focus of attention or behaviour, while maintaining a consistent level of response.

Assuming that something is going to happen during an interaction is probably the worst way to start it. The best way to proceed is to empty yourself of your priorities and try to figure out how your partner needs you 'to be', to recognise and enjoy your company. The most important achievement you are hoping for from the person is *involvement*. At this early point in the relationship you are learning to notice what the person may be communicating through their posture, activity and demeanour.

When working with a person who is familiar to you

As with the answer above, you are hoping to engage the person in a social exchange in which they find pleasure and comfort in the company of another human being. You are hoping to establish a level of acknowledgement, recognition, interest or involvement that can be revisited next time you meet. As the relationship emerges, you are also hoping to support them in their exploration of 'what might happen if I...?' that is, social cause and effect. It is crucial that the 'success' of an individual encounter, in the mind of the practitioner, is not time related, but connected with the degree of involvement.

It is hoped we will have more knowledge of a familiar person and their favoured behaviour, and you may have an emerging familiarity with certain activities that are favoured by them, that is the topics that seem to engage their interest, most of the time. Increased familiarity with these pathways of interaction can sometimes lead the practitioner to become less keenly observant of feedback and client or person inspired/directed variations. However, too much 'conscious' thinking can sometimes be a bad thing; in modern day parlance it is best to be 'in the zone' with the person and be going with 'the flow'.

This balance between being 'watchful' and 'flowing' presents difficulties, but it is important to remember that it is the underlying repetitive structure of this approach that underpins the learning, not the individual exchange. The exploration and new learning that you are aiming to support tends to come when the person explores a novel (sometimes unintended) variation in a familiar pattern, then enjoys and finds out how to revisit it, to achieve the response that it caused from their communication partner.

How much direct mirroring should you be doing – and how creative can you be with this?

When working with a person who is unfamiliar or familiar to you

How much of any particular strategy to use, and how particularly to employ it is something that can only be made in the moment with the person themselves. If direct and very precise mirroring works in the current circumstances with the person, then that is all right, and of course you can offer 'variations' on the current theme, to see how well they might be received. A considered blend of very direct mirroring of vocalisations or body movements and subtle variations (or sometimes quite dramatically different but still related responses) can work well, and if the person's attention wanders off or is redirected away from you, then you can always go back to very obvious mirroring and thus attempt to regain their attention.

There are times when you can use a creative variation, but being overly creative with the purpose of demonstrating your own ability as an imaginative interactor *is to miss the point of attempting to engage with the person in the first place.* Any wish to be creative should always be tempered by the need to negotiate a joint acceptance of any new variation used as part of a mirroring strategy. With more experience of both the person you might be working with, and of extended use of Intensive Interaction more generally, you do tend to develop a 'feel' for when to vary a mirroring behaviour and also by how much. But the same issue still applies – you continue to look for the feedback from the person to see if they still recognise any creative variations, and whether they are positively responsive to it – and if that is not the case then it is time to go back to the obviously recognisable point where you started to use variation.

Other issues that you may need to consider

One issue that should be carefully reflected upon is how or even whether to mirror back any behaviour that might potentially be self-injurious, for example when people might repeatedly tap, slap or even hit a part of their own body, or even knock parts of their body against a wall or parts of some accessible furniture. *Any mirroring response to this kind of behaviour should only be attempted with the utmost care, and with full approval and support of others involved in the care of that person.* That does not mean that mirroring such behaviour is necessarily wrong, or that it might not work in creating a sense of sociable interactivity that might eventually reduce the frequency or force of such a behaviour (and there is some anecdotal evidence that the outcomes of sensitive and reflective mirroring can reduce the impact of such self-injurious behaviour, e.g. Irvine in Firth *et al.* 2010, p.42). However, in such circumstances it is always necessary to seek advice from others, including any involved professionals, before proceeding, and any use in such circumstances would require extensive recording (preferably using video) and extensive collaborative discussion and reflection on the effects and continued use of such a technique. Such discussions should, whenever possible, be carried forward within a responsible multi-disciplinary team of experienced professionals charged with care or support of the individual.

Generally in such circumstances, the actual or potential self-injurious behaviour is not directly mirrored, but some related aspect of the behaviour, such as its rhythm, is reflected back in another way, for example via an associated rhythmical vocalisation or even a gentle clapping out of the behaviour's rhythmic pattern. It is preferably done at a slower and even gently decreasing tempo, so that any acknowledgement of the offered communication results in a decrease in tempo and vigour of the original behaviour enacted by the person themselves. If any attempt at mirroring aspects of challenging behaviour results in an increase in tempo or of vigour/force, then it should be immediately discontinued and another interactive strategy attempted, or the session temporarily curtailed.

What if the person gets bored of repeated routines – how would you recognise this and what could you do about it?

When working with a person who is unfamiliar to you

If you are asking this question then you are clearly attending to the interactions and comparing the person's involvement in relation to other interactions over a short time – well done! Although remember, we are discussing someone who is unfamiliar to you, and thus you do not really have a lot of insight into 'reading' the person yet. But you may have noticed their attention drifting off; they may have physically moved or turned away. If you are asking this question, you perceive that your partner might be uneasy, bored or anxious; or indeed you might be getting the impression that they are cooperating or going along with you rather than enjoying the interaction.

Your first strategy should be to record some video or to ask someone to watch you as you interact, to confirm that you are interacting with your partner based on behaviours they can recognise as their own, or that you are not missing anything in the person's responses that may be negative. At such an early stage in the process, a lack of interest is most likely to indicate that the person doesn't yet recognise that you are responding to them or doesn't understand or take any interest in what you are offering to them – so re-look at your observations and reconsider your interactive responses. The person may not recognise your responses as being 'of' them, or it may be that when you are with them, you are too close, moving too quickly, responding too literally, or demanding too much of them.

If you have timetabled yourself or freed yourself of other activities for, for example, ten minutes so that you can socialise with the person, it is easy to fall into the mindset that the interaction will take a length of time that will conveniently fall within those time boundaries. If the interaction goes on for longer than you allowed for, you might begin to feel pressure. If the interaction is much shorter, it is easy to assume that something went wrong. If the person repeatedly seems interested initially, but then becomes distracted or apparently bored, *then you might simply have discovered the length of interaction that suits the person most, that is they enjoy short interactions*. Once you have realised this you can go on to accommodate this and possibly offer a sequence of shorter episodes of interactivity sequenced with deliberate 'down times' that allow the person to rest or recover.

Other considerations to verify might include checking whether they are more interested in your social approaches in a different setting or at a different time; whether a different, much anticipated activity is just about to happen, or is happening somewhere else in the room; or even whether someone, who is for some reason distracting to your communication partner, is in the room with you.

When working with a person who is familiar to you

Assuming that you now have established some interactive and mutually responsive sequences of activity, which frequently revisit or follow similar routines, then it can also be assumed that you recognise or have begun to recognise the dynamics of how the person enjoys being engaged.

The first consideration is then: 'is it the person who is bored… or is it me?'

If it *is* you, then you need to focus on what you are doing and consider the person's social isolation and quality of life. You might begin initiating interactions in different settings or at different times. As you are familiar to the person, they will presumably recognise you and your approach wherever it happens, and the new setting might open up new interactive possibilities. It is vital not to disrupt the familiarity and structure of interactions you share, but by now, new settings might indeed generate new possibilities.

It must be said that it is unusual for people with complex intellectual disabilities and severe communication impairments to get bored in the presence of one of the few aspects of their life that responds consistently, memorably and enjoyably to their suggestions. However, if it is the person who is getting bored and you have confirmed that the causes are not attributable to anything in the previous section, you still have many possibilities. But first it is worthwhile to consider the following dynamic.

In the experience of someone with an intellectual disability and a severe communication impairment, the arrival of 'others' into their presence is frequently associated with the agenda that they (the person) will be expected to comply, cooperate or follow the suggestion of the person who has arrived. Staff routinely bring their own idea of 'what is going to happen next' with them, and expect the person to respond to it. While staff might bring an activity to 'compete' with the person, or take the person to a place to do something (albeit in a social setting), the person's role is that of recipient or compliance. Indeed, 'learned helplessness' (e.g. Seligman 1992) can be an insidious feature of the lives of many of the people we work with or care for – leading inflexible classroom timetables and daily activity schedules to be described as 'rotas for learned helplessness' by some in the field of special education.

During social exchanges in the style of Intensive Interaction, however, the person finds themselves in the unusual position of being the person *leading* the interaction rather than following the suggestion of the other person. While one of the strengths of the approach is that this reversal of roles is liberating and motivating to many people, for some it presents problems that they are not used to solving. Indeed that is very much the point: Intensive Interaction presents opportunities for the person to explore, practise and refine the skills associated with being a social agent, which can only be done in this active style of interaction.

Intensive Interaction is characterised by the person being supported to enter into open-ended interactions which are augmented and helped along by the responses of the skilled communication partner. Learning to recognise and explore responses and behaviours, establishing conventions and revisiting the invitations that lead to interactions is unknown ground for many of the people you might work with. *While the person might look bored or uneasy to the practitioner, it might well be that they are temporarily at a loss for a familiar route out of the pause that they find themselves in.*

While the introduction of 'objects' or 'resource items' can often resolve this problem, it may actually be ill-advised as the interaction may default to an interaction about the object. It is much more important and valuable for you to support them to find an interactive strategy from which to continue a purely social exchange. So how is this accomplished? It is accomplished by the skilled partner being playful and supportive.

If the interaction seems to stall, be patient, give the learner a chance to decide what to do next, that is, don't rush to suggest anything at first. If the stall leads to the collapse of an interaction (i.e. your partner walks off) remember this for the next time and watch closely in the interactions which follow to see if the same thing happens again. If it does, suggest a related but 'different yet familiar' focus of activity, using extended pauses and facial expressions to see if the person is interested in exploring this topic. Use an activity or format that you have visited together before, or an activity you have previously and frequently observed your partner being involved in; you might also suggest a change of activity from the previous one that seemed to be becoming boring. However, it is crucial that the practitioner does not insist that their suggestion is followed, and hands over the lead as soon as the person responds.

In some settings, practitioners and clients or learners can develop well-established interactive repertoires that do begin to become formulaic over years of daily contact. However, this usually worries the practitioner a long time before it concerns the person, who generally revels in the consistency, familiarity and controllable stimulation that interactions provide in a frequently boring day. If you are in an established interactive relationship, it is valuable to capitalise on the value of the 'well trodden paths' you have explored together. Use 'pausing' in your contributions and responses; waiting and 'teasing out' hesitation to see if the person takes control; urging or leading you to act. Experiment with tempo and levels of boisterousness or jovial fun. Introduce surprise, which, with repetition, sets the scene for anticipation and yet more hesitation, to extract as much mutual regard and shared pleasure as possible.

At the risk of sounding predictable though, if you are becoming uncertain of your responses, get some video and canvas the opinion of others involved with the person. Discuss the strategies you use and learn from the Intensive Interaction 'Community of Practice' that should surround you.

Can you try something a little different to see how the person responds – if so, when and how, and what should it be?

When working with a person who is unfamiliar to you

When interacting with someone new to you, everything you try will be novel. The aim for such an initial meeting is to try to develop an emergent rapport as the basis for future sessions, and so you should proceed with caution and try to develop a few strategies (or possibly only one) that successfully promote intensive interactivity. There is no rush to develop a wide range of strategies in a first encounter with someone (and even later on there is really still no rush), and so trying something 'different' should only have the aim of developing any emergent interactivity, and not of developing an interactive range within a session for its own sake.

However, if things are not going too well, and you are struggling or even failing to connect with the person, then you may feel that a change of tack might be required. If this is so, you should still follow the normal conventions of Intensive Interaction, and as such look for another way of responding to the things the person is currently doing, or use their current focus of attention as the basis of any interactivity. As an example, you might consider changing from a behavioural mirroring strategy to a verbal or vocal commentary on the person's behaviour, or somehow commenting on the current focus of their attention. It might also be possible that a change in your physical position relative to them might help, or changing the quality or your eye contact, or offering a burst-pause type of interactive game (e.g. a 'hide and re-appear' type of burst-pause activity).

Whenever trying something a bit different you should remember that you offer it tentatively to see the person's response. Then you will have to make a judgement on how long to persevere with a current strategy while it apparently receives little or no response, and when to cease and possibly try something new again. Whenever you consider such a change of tack it is always necessary to balance the need of the person to have time to take in any attempts at interactivity and garner some kind of sociable response with the need to find a means of connecting successfully. Rushing through a whole catalogue of interactive strategies in search of a 'magic interactive bullet' will almost always prove counterproductive. Patience, especially in these early stages, is a vital strategic element. Consciously employing a reasonable and inviting tempo to any tentative interactivity is generally prudent and allows the other person time to take on board what you doing, and then to find some kind of reasonable interactive response.

When working with a person who is familiar to you

When you are working with someone who is familiar, different interactive routines and games tend to develop naturally over time. These are mostly adaptations from and derivations (or even combinations) of what has worked before, and ideally will be based on some variation in the interactive behaviour of the person you are working with.

However, there are times when things happen that suggest a different interactive direction for a number of reasons (e.g. new observations of the person's behaviour, new interpretations of the person's behaviour, personal intuition, uninvited outside distractions or interference, and other possible variations of chance). New interactive routines do develop in the light of new, and sometimes more extended observations of the person's interactivity. This is part and parcel of the normal development of Intensive Interaction over time, and although mostly Intensive Interaction is a rational response to a person's interactive or emergent social behaviour, there are times when something new just seems to be the right thing at the right time. Sometimes your own latent or possibly intuitive creativity can take you along an interactive path that perhaps even surprises you, but nonetheless seems ideally suited to the person and the moment and therefore works well without the usual necessary rational reflective process.

The use of an intuitive interacting strategy seems to vary very much with the personality of the interactor, and unquestionably different practitioners demonstrate a range of degrees of intuition in their working practices. However, it wouldn't seem unreasonable to conclude that usually when any of us respond intuitively within a period of Intensive Interaction and it is successful, we are in fact responding according to the usual conventions of Intensive Interaction, but are somehow bypassing our own more conscious and organised thought processes.

Intuitive responding is in all probability not at all a random process, but is almost certainly well grounded in your previous interactive experiences. If you do arrive at some novel interactive means, you should always spend some time reflecting on the activity you chose; what you thought was actually going on, and why you think it worked. Even if you do have moments of successful interactive epiphany, Intensive Interaction is still, in the longer term, a rational process, and so you should always reflect on and further develop such moments of intuitive realisation.

So if you do feel that it is the right time to try something 'a bit different', initially do so tentatively, base it on good and continuing observations of the person's behaviour, but occasionally be open to more intuitive moments of creative responding. Always try to be aware of any changes in the environment, both social and physical, as these might explain different observations of the person's behaviour, and thus suggest possible novel interactive methods or routines. But as always, follow the person or join in with their current behaviour – you should never try to be creative to demonstrate your own interactive abilities.

Do you still have the necessary resource items available?

When working with a person who is unfamiliar to you

As the person is unfamiliar to you and you to them, you don't really know the circumstances in which they may discard an item in favour of something else. Use your observations to identify a time or setting when the person is at their least involved or dependent on any such object or resource item, to work with them interactively. Try to ascertain whether the object is being used as something to distract the person's attention away from worrying nearby events or people who make them anxious.

As was discussed earlier, it is usually best not to involve a resource item in an interaction, but if a person is inseparable from an item and never lets it go, then accept it as an aspect of who they are, and try to focus your responses on their other repertoires – sounds, qualities of movement or passing glances towards you.

When working with a person who is familiar to you

If, after prolonged attempts at interaction, you are finding it impossible to even intrigue their attention away from an item, it might be worthwhile finding yourself a version of it and using it in a manner which will be recognisable to the person, imitating the rhythms, movements and pauses they use. This might relax the person, and you may even be able to open up the option of offering to swap yours with theirs (a game which at a later time might be extended by then hesitating/offering the incorrect item/etc.). After several interactions based on your studious reflection of the person's activity, in which you imitate, reflect and/or burst-pause with the item, you might intrigue their attention by 'doing it wrong'. Whenever possible though, try to do without the item, as it can complicate matters and can lead to interaction about an *object* rather than interaction with and about *each other*. If you do use an object or resource item then use it as a tool to enhance opportunities for shared recognition and acknowledgement.

Experience shows that if a person demonstrates an emotional dependence on an object or the rituals attached to objects that this reliance will decrease as they draw increasing comfort and enjoyment from the increased opportunities to engage in understandable interaction with people. Many people have sought comfort from their activities with objects because the object is controllable and wholly reliable, whereas they cannot engage, influence or understand the people around them.

How will you know if you have achieved something worthwhile?

When working with a person who is unfamiliar or familiar to you

This will very much depend on what you think is 'worthwhile' each time you engage, or attempt to engage, interactively with someone. For an experienced interactor, every attempt at Intensive Interaction, whether successful or otherwise, provides new insights into the behaviour of the person, of any strategies that work, and also possibly of some that do not. Such observations should increase a practitioner's confidence in how exactly they should be working interactively with a person and highlight some strategies that might be discarded for the moment. There should also be an increased sense of joint familiarity between the participants of any attempted interaction, and that can only be of help in the longer term. If nothing else comes from a session of Intensive Interaction, then increased knowledge and increased familiarity alone should be seen as 'worthwhile' outcomes in themselves.

Other issues that you may need to consider

If you are supporting a practitioner or colleague who will be watching your session, to develop Intensive Interaction skills, it might be valuable to explain your general aims, thoughts and feelings to them prior to the interaction. Part of your Intensive Interaction work should be to carry other people with you and build the Intensive Interaction community around the person. Therefore you should actively be looking to identify, communicate and record the outcomes (and thus the worth) of all your Intensive Interaction work to others who can also work this way.

When considering the worth of using Intensive Interaction you can also look at the published research evidence to support your claims of the effectiveness of the approach. When employed as a structured and sustained approach, Intensive Interaction has been repeatedly shown to deliver enhanced or even novel interactive responses by the child and adult participants in structured research projects (see Chapter 5 for the full current list).

How long have you got left – is it going to be long enough?

When working with a person who is unfamiliar to you

One particular issue to beware of is losing track of time and being forced into having to come to an abrupt end due to drinks, meals or a taxi home. Time often disappears when you are focusing intently and so, especially in the early stages of your interactions with someone unfamiliar, try to ensure that they terminate with you rather than the other way around, as this gives the person with a social or communicative impairment ultimate control. So if possible give yourself flexible time boundaries, or prepare your colleagues for the fact that you might take a couple of minutes longer than expected. Explain why.

If you simply *have* to be somewhere else in five minutes, either go to your appointment early or do something else that uses your time wisely, for example do some more observation. If you feel it is appropriate, that is, that it is not you personally that the person is enjoying, but the interaction itself, you might arrange with someone to take over from you. Remember this is a team effort and the more people who know how the person communicates and can interact with them, the better.

When working with a person who is familiar to you

As you get to know each other, you might find that the person will, if given the chance, engage with you interactively for the entire day. In this case it might be advantageous to work with them in the knowledge that something equally or even more interesting than you will occur soon, for example drinks, meals or taxi home, and the person will leave you in favour of that distraction.

In general though, once you are familiar with a person and them with you, you will both acquire an understanding of what 'the end' looks like as it approaches. You may have established a 'convention' between you, or you might have noticed that the person's pauses become more prolonged as they become tired, and you can take advantage of this. If you know you are pressed for time before you engage a person, you might take a (hidden) favoured item or object of reference with you when you go to engage them, so that as you get to the end of your free time, you can introduce the item or activity which you know will distract their attention from you.

Remember that if you feel you are going to overrun the time you have, it is important to negotiate flexible times with colleagues who may be waiting for you.

How do you disengage with the person if it is going well and they really want to continue?

When working with a person who is unfamiliar to you

When a period of Intensive Interaction has been going well, even on the first occasion with someone, it can sometimes feel awkward or even somehow plain wrong to suddenly disengage or stop a successful sociable interaction. It might prove difficult for the person with a social impairment because they want the interaction to keep going, especially if it is enjoyable, or in some other way rewarding, and perhaps don't understand why it should end. It can therefore be helpful to think about using a deliberate disengagement strategy, such as deliberately slowing down the tempo of any interactivity to the point where it naturally peters out, or to redirect the person into some other activity that they then carry on alone.

It might be useful to consider a range of disengagement strategies that may be adopted if finishing a session of Intensive Interaction becomes difficult. Such strategies might be as simple as saying 'one more time' or 'thank you' or even 'okay' to someone who might understand such a use of language. For other people, appropriate disengagement strategies might include slowly decreasing the tempo of an activity, and at the same time slowly increasing the length of any pauses within it, eventually reaching a point when the interactivity naturally just comes to a close. Another strategy is to arrange for something else to happen just as the allotted time for the Intensive Interaction has expired, and this could be something as simple as a cup of tea or snack of some sort, or lunch being served, or the arrival of an escort or taxi home.

When working with a person who is familiar to you

When working with a person who is familiar to you, and with whom you share recognisable routines, the development of a 'final game' strategy could be considered. Such a strategy could employ the deliberate introduction of a recognisable activity that is repeatedly used as 'the last activity', that is, just preceding, and thus deliberately signalling the end of a session so that disengagement doesn't come as an unsignalled surprise. Such a 'last activity' should probably be a more leisurely paced activity that will reduce the arousal levels of both participants, as this can ease disengagement, and it might even include putting any resource items away, or moving slowly into another room.

Should Intensive Interaction be this easy or this hard?

When working with a person who is unfamiliar to you

This will depend on what you were expecting when you started, and what you think is easy and what you find hard. It is important not to compare yourself to training videos of expert or very experienced practitioners who seem to get a quick and easy response. It might work quickly, and it might not – we all have varying degrees of success, but you can be sure that the 15 minutes of video on the DVD was culled from at least four hours of unused footage. Video footage on DVDs is chosen to illustrate a point and does not represent the success rate you should expect as a day-to-day practitioner.

Acquiring any new skill tends to be the most difficult at the beginning. As you grow more experienced with a range of people, you will notice a fluency emerging in your practice. Your ability to be 'in the moment' yet watchful for people's rhythms, pauses and idiosyncrasies will develop. You achieve a cycle of watchfulness and real-time reflection involving:

- How are we going?

- How is the person feeling?

- How am I feeling?

- What am I focusing on?

- What is the person focusing on?

- What is the person responding to?

- Is this familiar?

- What might happen next?

- How did I respond last time?

How easy or hard any Intensive Interaction is will depend on a number of issues – time available, the support of other people, the person themselves, their character, their levels of isolation or passivity, possible mental health issues (e.g. depression), their mood and the time of day. Also be aware that the level of difficulty will reflect and be influenced by your mood and energy levels, and the degree of distraction coming from the environment.

Be very aware also, that it might be quite hard for the person too, who isn't necessarily used to interacting in this way and who may also be trying to figure out how to proceed and what to do with you. They might be wary of coming out of their familiar safe ground to interact with you. However, if it is going well for them, and you are achieving your objective of being a fluid and playful partner, they will spend most of the interaction simply enjoying the emerging familiarity and available control of the shared activity.

When working with a person who is familiar to you

Sometimes a run of previously unsuccessful Intensive Interaction sessions might affect your confidence as a practitioner, which might have a depressive effect on how you approach a person or how long you persevere – try to treat each interaction as you would a walk in the park – that is, you are now in largely familiar territory but there are a number of possible pathways you might be taken along, including standing still and enjoying the view.

You may have encountered worrying or challenging behaviour in previous interactions – consider what went wrong and adjust your approach, as the chances are you did something too much, too close, too fast or too suddenly. If you have encountered behaviours you find challenging, try to ensure you video the next couple of interactions to see if you can identify what set it off. Challenging behaviour, or any behaviour for that matter, does not just 'happen', although any causes of such behaviour may be *very* subtle (and therefore not easily observable) and possibly internal to the person (and therefore not observable at all).

It should get easier with familiar people in some senses, but not in others. While it gets easier to read someone or predict what the shape of the interaction will be, it is impossible to predict what might happen in *this* interaction. Practitioners often get to a point in their relationship with a person when they ask '*what is the next level?*', '*where should I be taking this?*' – the answer is that there is not a next level – Intensive Interaction is about what the person wants to do or is able to contribute, not what you want them to accomplish.

Practitioners tend to get accustomed or satiated with a style or pattern of interaction long before the person, who has spent their life unable to interact or recognise the social consequences of their behaviour, until now. There is no point trying to make an interaction more complex or making your contributions more subtle or logical (to you) or indeed more entertaining (to you), as you may well lose the involvement of the person. Remember that you are synchronising yourself to the person's style and speed of learning rather than leading the way or setting out what your partner will learn. Your world picture and understanding about social exchanges is complex and interconnected, so while you might know what you want to achieve, the person is still establishing the consistency of the connections between what they do and what you do.

Even when it is going well, Intensive Interaction should be effortful. It takes effort to arrange your time to manage the most flexible amount of time you have available. It takes effort to free enough of yourself mentally to temporarily discount the other tasks you might have to accomplish during the day, for example other routine care or support duties, other people's demands, managing other staff, doing rotas, etc. Intensive Interaction certainly takes cognitive and emotional effort to get it right in terms of good observation and responding reliably and consistently. If it feels totally easy, then you are probably not being observant, reflective or analytical enough. Spend more time watching yourself on video, or better still, get someone to watch some video of you interacting and ask them to give you some feedback on their impression of what has happened.

CHAPTER 3 What to Do and Think About After Using Intensive Interaction

Irrespective of the setting you work in, reflection is closely linked with good practice. It is well worth the effort to recap the main events of an interactive episode and note them down, all the while considering 'what was significant?' It might be useful to think about the interactive behaviours that you observed from the person you were working with, and you might also want to think about how you behaved and what you did, and what you both felt about any interactivity.

There is a wide range of recording formats and styles, some of which rely simply on a Dictaphone or quick note. Some examples of recording sheets that might be useful can be found in the appendix, and you can find others in other Intensive Interaction books, for example *A Practical Guide to Intensive Interaction* (Nind and Hewett 2001).

What did you do to engage the person – what techniques did you use and what have you learned from this session?

When working with a person who is unfamiliar to you

Although initially your actions will have been guided by your observations of the person with a communicative or social impairment, once you are interacting, you will usually be improvising and responding fluidly and 'in the moment'. As well as being observant of, and responsive to the interactive, or potentially interactive behaviours of the person you are trying to engage, you should also be critically reflective of your own interactive or potentially interactive behaviours after any Intensive Interaction session. Looking back analytically but constructively over what has happened (or what perhaps you expected or wished for but didn't happen) will certainly be time well spent. However, you should avoid the often natural instinct to look negatively or judgementally at your attempts or at the behaviour of your interactive partner.

Taking some time aside, either individually or with a colleague or supportive friend or family member, to recap and try to record what went on will undoubtedly pay dividends in the longer term. If the session was videotaped, then watching it and critically analysing the video would be even more enlightening and useful, to inform future attempts at Intensive Interaction with the person.

When you do look back analytically at your attempts (sometimes very successful, sometimes less so) at engaging the person, what exactly should you be trying to be analytical about? What are the techniques you can especially observe, analyse and record? Consider the following:

- How was the person behaving initially, and what response did you give back to them?

- Were you truly responsive? Did you really let them lead, or did you try too hard and end up taking too much control? Was there too much of your own usual social behaviour evident? Were you inadvertently defining too much of the interaction yourself?

- Were you in the right place, not too near but not too distant, too high or too low? Were you on the best side for someone's natural point of focus? Did you 'give good face'?

- What kind of tempo and rhythm did you use in your response, and did this match that of the other person?

- Did you successfully acknowledge the person in a way they could recognise? Did you affirm them with positive facial signalling and positive tone of voice/vocalisations?

- Were there any emerging patterns or sequences of behaviour that were revisited and repeated successfully during the Intensive Interaction?

- Did you use some kind of imitation or echoing response, and did this have the desired effect? Were you too 'loud' in your vocalisations or energetic in your movements, or too quiet and passive?

- Did you use any physical contact during the interaction, and if so was this too much or too little? Was any physical contact too static or overly dynamic?

- Did you use burst-pause strategies and build anticipation into the Intensive Interaction session? If so, how and when, and were these the right times and done in the right way?

- What emotional state did the person appear to be in at the start of the session, and did this alter in any observable way as the interaction progressed? If so, why might this have been?

Analytically and constructively reflecting on the issues listed above, preferably with a supportive colleague, friend or family member will be of definite benefit when you next attempt to interact with the same person. It will also help you develop yourself as a practitioner, and so will benefit other people who you wish to work with. Greater insight into your own interactive behaviour, and a structured and supportive exploration of your efforts at Intensive Interaction, will more certainly and more rapidly enhance your skills and confidence in this area.

When working with a person who is familiar to you

When working with someone who is familiar you should continue the process of critical reflection set out above, and repeated observations and subsequent periods of reflection (a process always enhanced with video evidence as this is more objective and often more accurate and comprehensive than our fallible memories). Regular periods of reflection will help you to be more accurate and insightful in your observations and subsequent evaluations, and without such a process, the development of successful Intensive Interaction will almost certainly be in some way compromised or delayed.

When you are familiar with someone, and a trusting relationship has been established around the repetition of familiar activities and interactive routines and games, you might also use the strategy of 'sabotage'. Thus, when you reflect on a session afterwards you might want to think about, and possibly watch any video taken of periods when we, as the skilled partner, might have purposefully responded incorrectly within the often repeated structure of a familiar routine or game – for example by not responding as expected, or simply doing something 'wrong', such as changing or delaying an expected vocalisation, sound or body movement. You might then wish to reflect on the response of the person to this unexpected change in the pattern:

- Does the person carry on regardless, or do they respond in some way indicating acknowledgement of the sabotage?

- Does the person try to 'repair' the interaction, and reclaim the familiar pattern, or do they understand the teasing nature of your actions?

- Does the person try to communicate something else to you when you sabotage a routine, for example by laughing or smiling?

Other issues that you may need to consider

While Intensive Interaction can simply be the sharing of time in a mutually enjoyable exchange, it is also important to be aware of your role as a communication partner with an interest in helping the person to acquire successful experience of social activity. Therefore looking back at the emotional aspects of the session (as well as the techniques used) can also be useful. You could ask yourself the following questions:

- How did the interaction seem for the person with a communicative and social impairment? Positive, or negative, or somewhere in the middle? And what makes you think this?

- Was the interaction mutually enjoyable or affirming, and were certain times or activities more enjoyable or affirming than others?

- How did it feel for you as a partner? Positive, or negative, or somewhere in the middle? And how confident did you feel about your attempts to engage the person during the session, and perhaps why did you feel this way?

How did you know if the person was ready for Intensive Interaction, and was this a good time to start a session?

The short answer is that assuming the person did not fall asleep or immediately get up and leave you, it was a good time. As practitioners you can learn something from any interaction and from the person's point of view, any social contact is better than none.

When working with a person who is unfamiliar to you

Taking into account the previous section, if you are feeling unsure about whether the person was ready for interaction, you might reflect on the information you could have got before approaching the person, for example *did other carers or people with a long association with the person suggest it was a good or bad time for the person to start with Intensive Interaction in terms of their mood or potential receptiveness?*

Generally though, with someone unfamiliar you will always be unsure of the best time to work, as this is something that generally comes with familiarity. However, again engaging in a process of analytic reflection might help you:

- What are the reasons you might have for feeling that this was not the best time?

- What indicators did you have that another time might have suited the person better?

- Were they tired? Were they hungry? Were they thirsty?

- Had they experienced a seizure just before or after the interaction? Might they have been uncomfortable from being in their chair too long?

- Were there any environmental distractions or time-related events (e.g. buses or taxis outside the window) or noises from others moving about or being within earshot, disrupting the flow of your interaction?

If the person you worked with seems happier, brighter or more peaceful, you know it was the right time for them, and discussion with others involved with them, video assisted reflection or your consideration of what went on during the interaction will tell you whether there were any lessons to be learnt for next time you try.

When working with a person who is familiar to you

The process of becoming familiar with your communication partner will gradually refine your judgement as to the best time and set of circumstances to work with them. The experience of different ways of working will constantly refine your understanding of the crucial factors that make one interaction flow and another stall. This is where keeping records of interactions is very important. While there are suggested recording formats in the appendix of this book, it is always important to develop your own method or regime of recording so that the information that is important for you to know, gets included. Having a record rather than a vague impression of how the interaction went is immensely valuable as our memories are very fallible.

How did you approach the person – what did you do first, and how was this received?

When working with a person who is unfamiliar to you

When wishing to reflect on how you initiate a session of Intensive Interaction there are a number of questions you can ask yourself that might throw some useful light on what was going on. You can identify what went well, and at the same time reflect on things you might wish to alter and do differently in the future. The kind of questions listed below will provide you with evidence of how you make yourself available for interaction with the person, and how you physically present yourself.

You could usefully ask yourself:

Did the person have sufficient time to adjust to your presence before you started?

Sometimes people with a social or communicative impairment might need a period of time to come to terms with your presence, and possibly come to realise something about your intentions. The person may need time to feel comfortable with you nearby and possibly will need time to realise that you do not wish to control or direct their behaviour. They might possibly need time to become curious about your intentions and your current activity (or lack of activity). Did you sufficiently account for these possibilities?

Did you wait for them to enter your space or did you enter their space?

The act of entering someone else's personal space can be, and usually is, a completely different issue to letting them enter your own. Actively going into someone's personal space can cause anxiety for some people with social and communicative impairments, and it can even at times be interpreted as threatening. In such cases it can cause some people to withdraw or even become physically challenging. Therefore you will need to proceed carefully with issues of proximity, and try not to be overly taxing on the person's toleration of you being physically close to them. You might need to move slowly and in a controlled or physically limited manner, and possibly even keep physically low down (preferably below eye level, sometimes even kneeling down or shuffling on your bottom towards someone in a chair) to make this process easier for the person to accept.

Another idea is to be sitting or standing quietly in a place that someone often frequents (i.e. deliberately positioning yourself in a place they frequently visit) before they arrive, and this can be one way of entering someone's personal space in a non-aversive manner.

Did you have to try to get an invite or were you welcomed in?

While you are actively trying to make an initial contact you will have to be extremely observant of the person's behaviour to notice what are often very subtle, short-lived, or tentative signals of acceptance or curiosity. Such a signal might be seen as a change in the person's visual focus to include you, possibly including some initial eye-contact; it might be signalled by a physical repositioning of the person towards you, possibly coming to sit or stand near by you, or even right next to you; or it might be signalled by a change in the tempo of, or a cessation in a stereotypical behavioural repertoire, as if waiting for you to do something (possibly even join in). Sensitivity to such potential signals, and catching such moments will obviously help you to engage with your communication partner.

Did you pick up on the game they were playing? Or did you pick up on the wrong thing and so missed the real game they were having with themselves until later in the interaction?

You could ask yourself whether your initial presentation was sufficiently associated with the person, or their current focus of attention. Although some people ostensibly seem to be engaged in a particular type of observable behaviour, it might just be a subtle aspect of that behaviour that you need to acknowledge or to offer something associated with it, as a social response. Finding which, if any, of a person's current behaviours might be the basis of a successful initial interaction can be a trial and error process, although extended experience of using Intensive Interaction can provide you with a more keenly attuned intuitive sense about how best to proceed in such circumstances.

Sometimes the biggest and most observable behaviours that someone is currently demonstrating (e.g. a full body rocking behaviour), are not the ones currently holding their attention; it might be a more subtle and less observable behaviour (e.g. thumb rubbing or squeezing within an enclosed hand) which might be the correct behaviour to attend to and respond to in some way. But sometimes getting it wrong is unavoidable, and so long as you are receptive to the person's feedback you should generally be able to rectify the situation quickly by moving on to another strategy.

Did you get close enough to the person?

You could well ask, how close is close? And of course this is a very subjective matter. As was mentioned above about being invited into someone's personal space, once you have been accepted in, you should still be aware of not pushing too far, too fast. People with social and communicative impairments might not respond too well to close proximity over an extended period of time, and they might need periods of downtime from close contact or proximity. Even then, they may still not want you to get too physically close to them, or accept any physical contact and indeed such a level of familiarity might be a long way off.

So again, you should proceed with caution, albeit a cautious optimism, in the earliest stages of developing successful strategies with the person you are attempting to engage in Intensive Interaction.

When working with a person who is familiar to you

Generally when you reflect on how you approached a person to engage them in Intensive Interaction you will ask yourself what you did and whether this seemed to work. As you get to know someone and the best means of interacting with them become increasingly apparent, you might then have a range of strategies or routines that you would be confident would elicit a positive response. This does not mean that you should cease to be reflective about how you present yourself or initiate periods of interaction, and the questions noted above might still be useful to ask.

Even with a person who is familiar to you, the person might still need a period of time to adjust to your presence. They may, or may not, still be anxious about people entering their personal space too quickly or forcefully; perhaps their positive experiences of proximity are still insufficient to make this process unproblematic for them, but you may be making some progress. It might be all right, but equally, more time might be required, and so you should remain optimistically cautious and observant for any early signs of rising anxiety.

Perhaps with increasing familiarity the person now recognises you and your intentions, and increasingly invites you to socialise with them and join in with their current behaviour or perhaps they might initiate some jointly recognisable interactive game or routine. However, people being people, we can all be victims of differing moods and preferences on different days and at differing times. You should never assume that the strategy that worked well the last time you were together will necessarily 'do the trick' this time. You will still need to be observant of the person's behaviour and their responses to you to gauge whether you have picked up on the correct form of response to them now, at *this* time. You will still need to engage your observation and reflective skills just as much even when someone is very familiar to you.

Other issues that you may need to consider

You should always remain open to changes and real progressive developments in the level of a person's communication abilities and their interactive preferences. You should make a priority to be sensitive to any developmental progress immediately, and be ready to move on and support any advances with developments in the level of sophistication of your responsiveness. However, you should not push for such developments and end up moving ahead of the person you are working with and beyond the level that is right for them. Thus, you should continue to assume plenty of repetition and need for familiarity in the early stages of any Intensive Interaction period (and at all other times actually), and this should be evident in the way you present yourself.

What new behaviours did you observe from the person during this session?

When working with a person who is unfamiliar to you

If the person is unfamiliar, all the behaviours may appear as new. If you have previous experiences of Intensive Interaction with other people, some or even many of the behaviours may look familiar in some way. However, do not fall into the trap of assuming that similar behaviours might mean the same thing or have the same function or intent to all the people who engage in them. To be a good practitioner of Intensive Interaction you need to suspend your assumptions about what might be pleasant, tedious, or scary. During a first meeting scenario you need to be keenly observant of the person's behaviour, locus of interest, tempo and body position, pallor and facial signalling, activity, eye contact, proximity, etc. Start to record what you see for comparison later on in the process.

Following your initial attempts to strike up a conversation or to capture the interest of the person it would be valuable to show video to others who are familiar with them to get their opinion (and involvement) about whether the person was interested.

You may be tempted to begin your next interaction by repeating some of the routines that you explored in the previous session – but beware of leading. In the early stages of familiarity you are still gathering observations and ideas and should still be keenly watching out for patterns, or for a style or response to emerge. Video is the most powerful tool you have to help at this point in your relationship.

A valuable exercise would be to record your impression of how the interaction went, including the initiations, any interactive routines or behaviours and any novelties that you recall. After you have done this, watch a video of the interaction you have just recorded and see what you forgot.

When working with a person who is familiar to you

While video is still the most powerful resource you have to assist comparison over time, and to identify new or emerging repertoires and routines, you will be developing a familiarity with the person's way of interacting and their regular pleasures and default repertoires. After an interaction it is very important to recall whether any old interactive routines were revisited, whether any old routines had 'new bits' and whether old routines have changed in some way over time.

There are *two* aspects of ascertaining whether anything new happened and both require video to get the most out of this reflective practice:

1. You might consider the *behavioural* aspect of what occurred, for example when I sabotaged an activity (e.g. clapped my hand instead of vocalising in a game of vocal call and response)

   (a) Was it too disruptive?

   (b) Were they curious to see what I'd do?

   (c) Did it restart flagging interest?

   (d) Did they try to get me to revert to the established game? (Did I miss this – i.e. did I miss that s/he was trying to redirect me/request something?)

(e) Did they enjoy what happened? (How do I know?)

(f) Did they persist with what they were doing...possibly meaning that they didn't recognise the difference in what I did, or possibly that they simply assumed it was a pause? (Thus did they re-take their turn?)

or

2. When the person did something new (e.g. vocalised and gazed at me) what was the precursor to them doing this?

(a) Was it something I did?

(b) Did something happen nearby?

(c) Was it a signal of something?

(d) What happened next?

    (i)   Did they try a new game?

    (ii) Did they continue along the previous path?

    (iii) Did they continue or was it only momentarily?

(e) How did I respond?

(f) What else might I have done?

When something does happen that might be novel for the person then you might ask yourself: 'Have I seen this before, and what were the circumstances?' and further reflection might take you to ask yourself:

- Was I prepared?
- What followed?
- How did I respond?
- Where did it lead?

You might also decide to look at the interaction at a structural level. Using the stages that make up the Framework for Recognising Attainment in Intensive Interaction (see appendix) you could identify the statement that sums up the interaction most accurately and compare this with previous records. The Framework identifies the *level of involvement* demonstrated by the person rather than the actual skill set used, and as such does not focus on the discrete exchanges that took place. This tool focuses on the nature of the interaction and functions of the person's communicative attempts.

Did you achieve what you hoped for, and was it worthwhile?

When working with a person who is unfamiliar to you

As stated earlier, your view on what you have achieved during any session of Intensive Interaction, and whether this was what you had hoped for, will very much depend on what it was that you had hoped for at the outset. Whenever we work with someone who is unfamiliar it can be difficult to form any insightful expectations of what might realistically be achieved. If you set out with relatively flexible and restrained expectations of what might happen, then anything positive that does happen will then have at least matched, and will in all probability have exceeded your expectations. It is important to remain positive in your reflections and look for attainments rather than failings (and as stated earlier, even passivity might be seen as a positive if it is not an outright rejection of your social availability). It might be useful to remember that the person has, in all reality, a lifetime to develop their interactivity; there is no rush in the initial stages to prove yourself as a practitioner or to get observable results. Intensive Interaction is a cumulative process and often an incremental one that moves forward slowly. If a session is the first Intensive Interaction someone has encountered, then the most worthwhile aspect is that it is the start of a process that will go on to reap rewards in the longer term, even if very little seems to have happened in the short term (although quite a lot can and often does change even in the short term).

Intensive Interaction can only be developed collaboratively, and so must move forward at the person's pace, and will only work with a person with a social or communicative impairment if it is practised in a way that is demonstrably 'on their terms'. The person's individual 'terms' might take some time and effort to work out, and they may need some time to get used to your presence and your attempts at interactivity. Moreover, they may need time to work out and come to trust your sociable and non-directive intentions.

Therefore you need to be sensitive and realistic in the short term, but relentlessly optimistic in the medium and longer term. So, when you reflect on what has just happened and what has been achieved, you should be analytical of your own Intensive Interaction practice, and not just critical. You should tease out the successes contained within any Intensive Interaction session that are worth celebrating. These successes might be at the level of: 'they fleetingly looked at me!' or 'they vocalised when I was near to them' or 'they let me sit next to them' or 'they stayed in the same room as me!' It might well be that such achievements are the very best that could realistically have been hoped for and so should be celebrated as positive outcomes, recorded as such and shared with colleagues, friends or family members.

Finally, it might also be useful to think of each session of Intensive Interaction as providing someone with a basic human right, that right being satisfied by you attempting to include them in a 'meaningful two-way communication' or social experience (as stated in the 2009 UK government document *Valuing People Now* (Department of Health 2009)). From such a basic 'inclusion' perspective, the very fact of you offering such an experience is in itself intrinsically worthwhile, no matter what the outcome, and really should not need any further justification.

When working with a person who is familiar to you

As stated previously, when you are working with someone who is familiar to you, you are more likely to have some ideas, however tentative, about what to expect during an interaction. You should be developing your ideas on which strategies and interactive routines are becoming well rehearsed and increasingly familiar. You should be developing your ideas on when and where to start a session of Intensive Interaction, how to present yourself initially when you wish to start, and the length of time over which Intensive Interaction works best for the person you are working with. However, you should always remain flexible in your expectations; different sessions will follow different paths, and for a variety of reasons some will go at different paces from previous sessions. A person's chosen means of interaction can and will at times differ, and a person's interactive level, in terms of its level of sophistication, may well progress or even on some occasions seem to regress. You might experience that previously successful strategies and routines have somehow drifted or developed, or perhaps they may just not have been 'the right thing' during the current session (although as previously stated, repetition is the main building block for familiarity and thus all progress).

When reflecting on a session of Intensive Interaction, you should not take the person's willingness to engage or their positive responses for granted. Subtle shifts in their mood or general preferences may have affected their willingness to engage in what have been well rehearsed and familiar routines. So a session may not have developed as expected, and it may not even have achieved previous levels of engagement, but it does not mean that a session was not worthwhile.

Intensive Interaction is a cumulative and most often incremental process (after any initial rapid expansion through the expression of a person's latent, but previously unused communicative abilities). Therefore each session is intrinsically worthwhile because any Intensive Interaction, at a most basic level, provides inclusive social opportunities that are part of a longer term process. There might even be some difficult times or even apparently 'backward' steps along the way, but it is up to you to remain sensitively realistic in the short term, and equally to remain relentlessly optimistic in the medium to long term.

Were you sufficiently observant of the person? Did they, or might they have done something you didn't see?

When working with a person who is unfamiliar to you

Early interactions are the most difficult as the practitioner is often so preoccupied with responding consistently and quickly that on reflection the memory of the exchange is vague. It is usual for most people to feel that they 'could have been a better partner'. But you can only do your best, and video footage or the eyes of another practitioner are always useful. Almost invariably the video will show something that you did not see – it is a product of the different viewpoint of the camera, and the wonderful facility that video cameras give you to stop time and have another look at something. In real time you respond to what you notice at the time and as with all interactions, your concentration on one aspect of your partner's behaviour may well lead you to miss other aspects.

When working with a person who is familiar to you

When working with someone for an extended period of time, it is noticeable that the new behaviours or contributions they make can often stand out more clearly from the 'known' range of repertoires routinely seen. '*Am I being I sufficiently observant?*' is actually a question that seems to be asked more in an established relationship than in a new one. Practitioners sometimes realise that they have lapsed into interacting with an increasing degree of habit or 'auto-pilot'. This can be especially problematic with a person whose range of disabilities results in them having a very limited range of interactive options open to them. The practitioner realises that interactions have been following a 'well trodden path' and believes that they must be missing some important communicative attempt in the process. Making a regular video record of interactions will identify whether you might be missing an obscured attempt to communicate.

This question is frequently asked around the same time as the '*what is the next level of interaction?*' question, and can often be associated with what is felt to be a levelling off of 'progress' in the interactions. Firth (2008) recognised that in the initial phases of Intensive Interaction, practitioners frequently noticed a diversification of communicative repertoires and rapid increase in the person's interactive attempts as latent and previously unregarded communicative skills are demonstrated during a period of Intensive Interaction. It is noted that for a variety of reasons, this apparent diversification eventually 'levels out' as the person seems to contribute fewer new strategies and apparently demonstrates a slower rate of progression or learning (for a detailed discussion of this phenomena see Firth 2008).

It is during this second phase that practitioners begin to feel that interactions are becoming repetitive, or that they are becoming less observant. Usually they are mistaken. It may be speculated that early exposure to Intensive Interaction allowed the person to find applications for what they had already learned from experience, while now, as learning appears to be slowing, they are actually at the cutting edge of their ability to understand and are busy in the business of acquiring and consolidating new learning.

Some people may well have acquired understanding or recognition of social cause and effect through experience of life, routines and learning about the consequences they perceive. However, they may have been unable to demonstrate this learning in the context of social interaction with professionals who can too often focus on training, compliance and resolving a person's perceived 'deficits'. But when the demands of social interaction are limited to 'that which the person already understands', and professionals use their skills to support the person's style of interaction in open-ended social encounters, rather than to demand conventional communicative styles, involvement becomes more achievable and the person's capacity for interaction emerges.

If you are worried about your observations, use video to capture regular samples of interactive exchanges. These will provide a record of progress and a resource for future reference.

Could you use some different resource items to better effect next time?

As previously noted, the use of resource items (or sensory objects) is something that you can keep in mind as a potential means of generating sociable opportunities, generally when a person clearly shows determined motivation to engage in such a focus. However, you should always be careful not to become dependent on objects, as this could lead to a form of parallel but individualised sensory exploration, that is, more 'doing alongside' someone than intensively interacting with them.

If you are working with someone who has a clear attachment to certain objects (or types of objects) then you might look to introduce something similar to the thing they already have. Having said that, it might well be better, initially, to try and be inventive in your use of any currently favoured objects; using them creatively but sensitively as a joint focus for your interaction. There should be no rush to introduce new routines or develop new games around such favoured objects, and any change to an established object focused routine should naturally develop from those that have previously been successful. Such developments might include subtle changes to the tempo, rhythm, vigour or movements (or volume if they generate sounds) previously seen to be used by the person with the objects, or perhaps employing a burst-pause holding back of something in a teasing or playful manner.

If you do think it appropriate to engage someone socially around a resource item or object, then you might usefully ask yourself if there are some variations on a theme possible with any objects that the person regularly likes (or needs) to have with them, for example something slightly different in form, size, shape or colour (or something that might be noisier or quieter). Consider how you might use these to help you to smoothly extend out an activity naturally into something that might be slightly different.

You may in fact work in a place that has access to a sensory room or setting, and thus there may often be some developmentally appropriate and often very expensive resource items around and visibly available for the person (or you) to pick up and explore. But you should guard against becoming too focused on their use, and it might well be better to ration the availability of such objects thoughtfully, as your aim is to engage the person socially rather than to meet their sensory needs. We would certainly acknowledge that a good understanding of a person's sensory needs or desires might be useful to you in refining your interactive practice to make it more suited to the person you are working with.

Another way to look at this issue is to ask yourself if there are suitable objects or resource items usually and more naturally and freely available in the immediate environment that might draw or hold the person's attention and be used within Intensive Interaction? If there are such items, then this is an area of sociable interactivity that can progress naturally, so long as it is still firmly based on the interests and behaviour of the person you are working with.

Other issues that you may need to consider

For some carers or staff, the regular use of resource items or objects can unintentionally lead them to be overly directive in an Intensive Interaction engagement. Some people seem to fall into wishing for a particular kind of 'correct' or 'culturally acceptable' use of the resource items. This can lead to staff or carers subtly supporting (or more often directing) the person to do something 'the right way' (i.e. their own preferred way) rather than following the person's lead and joining in with their way of using or exploring the object or item (which might contrast sharply from the original or usual use of the object).

Quite often it appears as if an object brings with it an invisible 'cultural framework' that then has to be adhered to once the object is taken up by the person with a social or communicative impairment. Shakers have to be shaken, drums have to be hit, balls have to be thrown or kicked, bricks have to be built up, buttons have to be pressed, magazines have to be looked at or read, paper has to be drawn upon, etc. But of course, those are our conceptual limitations based on, and constrained by, our own experiences. Such encultured limitations should be put to one side while you see what the person themselves wishes to do, or not do, with the particular objects. What aspects of the object do they find interesting and worthy of exploration? You should then see if you can follow their lead and possibly reflect back or comment in some positive way on their activity, and maybe also join them in their activity in some way that is sociable and supportive rather than becoming directive and culturally bounded.

Did you have long enough?

When working with a person who is unfamiliar to you

If the person walked away from you or spent time engaged with you then eventually lost interest, you had enough time. You know when you didn't have enough time because you had to leave when the person was definitely interested and engaged with you. Generally we all too easily assume that because we have a period of time for a 'session' that the interaction should fill that period to be acknowledged as productive. You cannot assume that the person will be interested in as extended an interaction as you, as they may not be able to focus the cognitive effort required for a prolonged interaction. Remember, any skill is hard work to accomplish in its early stages, especially when the person may be slightly confused by having someone close by without something tangible happening, as it generally does with other staff when they approach.

If you felt you have learned something useful and your communication partner enjoyed your presence – then yes, you had enough time.

When working with a person who is familiar to you

When you compare the interaction with a previous exchange, you might well reflect that it was shorter or less 'productive' than you had hoped. Remember that best practice of Intensive Interaction is person focused and the interaction follows the person's choice of route. Enjoy the interaction you had. Unless you were interrupted by an outside influence, or organisational necessity, which in hindsight you could have avoided, then you had enough time.

As you are familiar with the person, you should realise that:

1. some interactions are longer than others, depending on uncontrollable factors, including mood, comfort, interest, arousal and surrounding influences, including what happened ten minutes before you joined the person, and

2. the benefits of the approach are to be found in the cumulative effect of the emerging relationship being forged between the interactive partners rather than the individual interaction.

How did you disengage with the person?

When reflecting on a period of Intensive Interaction, it is sometimes useful to think about how you ended a session and disengaged socially from the person. You should perhaps ask yourself if it felt like the session came to a natural end-point, or ebbed away to a point that both parties seemed to acknowledge the session had run its course. However, you might also feel that the session's final moments felt somehow awkward or unsatisfactory for some reason.

Useful questions you could ask yourself might include:

- Did you give some useful indication of the imminent arrival of the final activity/game so that the end did not surprise the person?

- Did you deliberately slow the tempo down or slowly increase the length of any pauses within any interactivity, to the point where the session of Intensive Interaction naturally petered out?

- Did you introduce something at the end of the session that you knew would be a good distraction away from the Intensive Interaction?

- Did you redirect the person into some other activity that they could then carry on alone?

- Did you redirect the person into another supported activity of some sort?

- Were you cute enough and managed it so that something more interesting came along just at the end-point or time limit (e.g. a recess or break time, or a cup of tea or snack arriving, or lunch being served, or the arrival of an escort or taxi home)?

Other issues that you may need to consider

As mentioned earlier, for some people who struggle to voluntarily disengage, serious consideration might be necessary for the development of a 'final game' or deliberate disengagement strategy employing what will, it is hoped, in time, become a recognisable 'last activity' that deliberately signals the end of an Intensive Interaction session. Such a 'last activity' should almost certainly be a more leisurely paced activity, one that is deliberately designed to reduce the joint arousal levels and social attunement of both participants – indeed such a 'final game' or disengagement strategy could well include putting away any resource items, or both people moving leisurely into another room or onto another activity.

What was easy or hard about the session?

When working with a person who is unfamiliar to you

We generally find things easy when we identify solutions or skills to respond fluidly to a problem and we find things hard when we can't. If it was easy, congratulate yourself on what went well (even if it didn't go as well as you had wanted). If it was fun, even more congratulations are in order as, if you had fun, the chances are that your communication partner did too!

Recall the interaction and identify what you found difficult – distractions, interruptions, competing noises or finding responses to the person. If the difficulty was resource or personnel based there is always a solution. It might lie with room management, organisation or venue allocation. If the difficulty relates to finding ways to respond in a way that the person can discriminate, it might take more observation, consideration and discussion with someone else interested in the person or indeed, in this approach. Practitioners often find it difficult to find a response to a person if they perceive that the repertoires they see are destructive, aggressive or socially unacceptable – if this is the case, you should return to your observations and find people at a time when they are contentedly focused on something of their own choice – it is incredibly rare for someone to have the energy to be destructive, and aggressive all day. (If they *are* then addressing the causal factors is the priority – nearly all challenging behaviour has a communicative function.)

When practitioners find difficulty responding to the person's repertoires or communicative attempts because they seem odd or unconventional, they often benefit from the support of others around them engaging the person as well. Clearly if the person has the usual range of physical movement, the difficulty experienced by the practitioner might come from deciding which behaviours to respond to and what to ignore. It seems sensible to acknowledge any behaviour or attempt that your communication partner makes to involve or acknowledge you, by simply affirming it. If you have some way of responding to a repeatedly seen or idiosyncratic characteristic of the person's activity in a manner which will encourage them to elaborate on it, or use it to relate to you in any way, do it. If you don't have a response, then return to your observations and consider it, then refine it in the light of experience.

Caution should be used in relation to any formulaic use of imitation, echoing, burst and pause, sabotage and other 'techniques' that are frequently discussed in Intensive Interaction. These are terms used to describe the natural features and characteristics of the way we express our sociability. They are not techniques to deploy in a set-piece configuration. Communication is a fluid and intuitive process. However, for some reason the mindset which influences many 'staff' who communicate to 'clients' or people with intellectual disabilities is characterised by a power balance demonstrated by the 'commands' they use and the 'objectives' they devise. Intensive Interaction encourages you to interact with people with intellectual disabilities and communication impairments as communication partners with equal value. To sensitise practitioners to the processes which nurture emerging communication and underpin interaction, the approach places a microscope on the dynamic processes involved in communication. Hence we have coined a number of phrases which describe these processes. Do not use them rigidly or with any particular ratio of frequency – be fluid.

When working with a person who is familiar to you

Just like a chat with an old friend, passing time enjoyably together gets progressively easier and more contented as time passes. Often passing time together actually becomes the point of interacting, rather than joining any specific activity or performing a mutual function, so things might well seem easy, now that you are in an established communicative relationship. However, the practitioner's purpose is to be watchful and attentive. This is why regular reflection, discussion and recording are important. While you should not seek to hothouse or predict progress, you should seek to support its elaboration and monitor what happens so that others can learn how to interact with the person.

If you are having difficulty, do not take it personally. Communication is the most complex piece of learning that humans acquire, and we are endeavouring to help the people with the most complex cognitive problems to grow the confidence and understanding to be able to use it. Share the difficulty with others, ask others to help, and discuss the issues with colleagues or family members.

CHAPTER 4 Some Final Issues to Consider When Using Intensive Interaction

Consider what you can do to develop your own competence and confidence as an Intensive Interaction practitioner

If things are going well over the course of several sessions

Generally, and most often, if practised correctly and reflectively Intensive Interaction will proceed in a relatively straightforward manner, bringing increasing and cumulative rewards as successful interactive sequences and routines build up and relationships deepen. However, there are some general pointers below that will guide how best to continue to develop your own confidence and competence as an Intensive Interaction practitioner:

- Generally it is best to be open and transparent about what you do in your Intensive Interaction work – talk openly and frequently about your particular work, and about Intensive Interaction more generally, with anyone who is interested – and even with people who aren't particularly interested…but should be.

- Look back specifically on your recent Intensive Interaction work and list to yourself the successful interactions that have occurred, that would not have occurred without your active presence. Think positively about your own contribution to the enhanced social inclusion and the subsequent pleasure you have given to the people who you work with or care for – and don't be shy in pointing this out to others.

- Continue to reflect critically and constructively on your current Intensive Interaction practice, preferably using video of your current interactions to inform such reflections and analysis. There should never come a time when any of us can relax and think that we know it all, that we have all the answers, and that we no longer need to reflect on what we do and how we do it.

- Invite other people whose judgement you trust (and preferably people who are to some extent experienced in Intensive Interaction themselves) to observe your Intensive Interaction practice or collaboratively analyse video of your Intensive Interaction practice. Ask them to give you constructive comments and supportive advice about how to move forward from your current Intensive Interaction practice which they have seen. Do not be afraid to ask people if they see anything that they might legitimately question about your practice. Such an inviting and proactive type of question can help people be more open in their critique, and being transparent about areas that might genuinely need some reflection can only help all of us to become better at what we do. But try not to feel that any such professional criticism is meant personally, use any issue or constructively raised question to reflect on and try to improve specific areas of your practice.

- Make every effort to access all relevant Intensive Interaction training at the highest level applicable to your current circumstances, whether this is a one-day introductory presentation, a more involved and extended practice-based training programme, an advanced practitioner type course, right up to a more formalised Intensive Interaction coordinator type course (e.g. leading to accredited Intensive Interaction coordinator status).

- Continue actively to gather the most up-to-date information about both the theory and practice of Intensive Interaction: this can be achieved by reading any new books on Intensive Interaction, watching any new Intensive Interaction DVDs, subscribing to (and reading) the Intensive Interaction newsletters, regularly accessing Intensive Interaction websites or online networking groups, joining and attending any local Intensive Interaction support groups, or by any other means readily at your disposal.

- Continue to gather up-to-date information about any research that is published in academic or research journals, for example by being notified via the Intensive Interaction newsletters or Intensive Interaction websites. But also, depending on where you live or work, you could even actively develop contacts in a specialist library or with someone in an appropriate academic establishment.

- Perhaps you could also take some responsibility for teaching and supporting others to use Intensive Interaction; explaining, or trying to fully explain things to other people is always a good way of coming to understand an issue or concept more profoundly yourself. It is also a quick way to discover any gaps in your own understanding when trying to answer simple but often profound and probing questions from others who don't yet fully understand the same issue.

If things aren't going so well over the course of several sessions

If, for whatever reason, things aren't going too well in terms of your Intensive Interaction practice, then there may be some other things, as well as those listed above, that you might want to try. These might include the following points:

- It is often best to remember that Intensive Interaction can at times be a real 'trial and error' process – so it is simply not possible to get Intensive Interaction immediately right for everyone all of the time. Being too hard on yourself when things are not going according to your plan can be the worst possible response. Being overly self-critical or feeling a sense of 'failure', although often a normal human reaction to life's difficulties and frustrations, is often counterproductive, and can make any future progress more difficult to achieve. It is generally best to remain cautiously optimistic that any Intensive Interaction related problems can be and, with the necessary resolve and correct advice, will be overcome.

- In certain circumstances it might also be useful to seek some individual supervision with a more experienced Intensive Interaction practitioner to explore the particular difficulty you are encountering. Open and frank supervisory discussion can help objectify any particular difficulty, and may give you a new perspective on the issue. Such a discussion may point you to a different way forward in terms of the practical use of the various Intensive Interaction strategies, or it may reassure you that you are doing all you can in the current circumstances (e.g. if a problem is more systemic or managerially related than individual or practice related).

- For some people more professional models of supervision are not available, but it might be equally useful to have a more informal chat with someone and air your particular concerns or feelings about any difficulties that might be confronting you. Sometimes the old adage 'a problem shared is a problem solved' (or is it 'halved') is an accurate representation of the release or relief sometimes achieved by taking advantage of such an informal social support mechanism. However, if you do have an informal chat about any Intensive Interaction related issues, choose the right people who will have the right temperament, the necessary interest and necessary time to do so successfully.

If things are going badly wrong (for whatever reason) over the course of several sessions (or even within one particular session of Intensive Interaction)

If, for whatever reason, things start to go badly wrong in terms of your Intensive Interaction with someone with severe or profound and multiple learning difficulties and/or autism (possibly due to a person's resort to challenging or self-injurious behaviour), then there may be a requirement that you take a step backwards. It should never be your intention as an Intensive Interaction practitioner that you affect any activity that might in some way have a negative or harmful impact on the person you are working with or caring for. In the rare event that things go wrong in some respect when using Intensive Interaction (and this can certainly happen when working with people who exhibit certain challenging behaviours) then the best advice is generally to physically distance yourself, make yourself and the other person safe and if necessary, discontinue the current use of any Intensive Interaction techniques. It might well be possible to re-engage someone with Intensive Interaction after just a few minutes, although some people may need considerably longer before any further attempts at engaging them socially are restarted.

In all such instances a thorough critical analysis of what might have gone wrong, or what might have seeded a particular response, should be carried out. This certainly doesn't mean that you should stop using Intensive Interaction with the individual concerned, but it does mean that you might have to re-evaluate how you practically employ the approach. Any such re-evaluation is generally best done transparently with any other people who might use Intensive Interaction or work in other ways with the person concerned. Certainly details of any untoward incident should be shared with someone who is responsible for the care of the individual or who has any managerial authority over the relevant service (and this may require the completion of any necessary forms or paperwork).

Once you have stepped back, and reported any such incidents then your re-evaluation of the Intensive Interaction process and the practices thus employed can start. This re-evaluation is best undertaken by employing one of the above mentioned supervision or collaborative analytic processes. Thinking critically yet constructively about what might have happened, and what might have caused such an instance to happen, should help you to go some way to learning from and resolving such an issue. At the very least you should adapt your practice to make any such incident less likely to happen, or if any such incident does continue to occur you should look to work in a way that will ameliorate any potentially harmful effects.

Consider how other people can be productively involved and supported in developing successful Intensive Interaction

If things are going well over the course of several sessions

You can work far more effectively in a team than you can alone; actively plan to work collaboratively with colleagues as they can provide insights from their particular perspective, which is always valuable. They can hold video cameras for you, can confirm that what you think is happening is actually happening, or re-assure you that it is not. But most of all, once informed about how and where to interact, colleagues can begin to interact with the person as well, giving them more interactive partners and more experience of the slight variability in responses that inevitably occur when they interact with someone other than you.

INFLUENCING COLLEAGUES WORKING DIRECTLY WITH YOU

If you want to encourage your direct work colleagues to use Intensive Interaction with you and you haven't got much experience or knowledge yourself, but see the value of the approach; consider the following:

- You need good information. Get a book or training DVD – there are many publications about Intensive Interaction available from bookshops, Intensive Interaction websites and Internet bookshops. You might also download some articles on the approach (see www.intensiveinteraction.co.uk, www. drmarkbarber.co.uk or www.leedspft.nhs.uk/our_services/ld/ intensiveinteraction).

- You should certainly attend some training; there are a range of courses advertised on or through the websites already mentioned and there are free Intensive Interaction newsletters published in UK and Australia (see Further Reading section for details). Other commercial training organisations also offer Intensive Interaction training, and these are generally advertised on the Internet and a Google search of 'Intensive Interaction training' might alert you to some of these.

- It might be valuable to join one of the local Intensive Interaction networks, and again details should be available via the above mentioned websites, or you might suggest that your organisation invites an accredited training provider to your workplace.

If you have already started using Intensive Interaction and you want to encourage your direct work colleagues to use the approach with you, you might consider the following in addition to the above:

- The best way to encourage colleagues to try Intensive Interaction is by demonstrating good practice yourself. Make sure you take every opportunity to do so when your colleagues are watching. Make it a public act wherever possible. The person's interest in you, their desire to engage you, and your clear enjoyment of the exchange, will act as a catalyst for discussion.

- It might be best to get some video of yourself and the person who you have been working with, and use this to introduce the approach to colleagues. If you are not confident to do that yet, use video from the instructional DVDs that are available (e.g. *The Intensive Interaction DVD* by Dave Hewett (2006), *Learning the Language* by Phoebe Caldwell (2002), or *Exploring the Envelope of Intensive Interaction* by Mark Barber and Karryn Bowen (2009)) and then discuss how you went about applying the principles discussed to interactions with the person you are working with. However, experience certainly shows that it is very powerful to show video of individuals that your audience already know. The best possible scenario is that you have a range of video vignettes showing the person's interactions with others before you started; your first interactions, and then later footage which shows the person exploring your responses.

- Give your colleagues information about the approach; there is an excellent free download from www.bild.org.uk (at www.bild.org.uk/pdfs/05faqs/ii.pdf) that provides an independent and basic description of Intensive Interaction. You may already have some resources from your own search for information – distribute these, or collect them together into a dedicated Intensive Interaction file freely available for others to access.

- Encourage colleagues to watch you and help you to take video, so that you can watch it together and discuss what you are doing, and if you are in a position to do so, arrange some periods in the day when they can begin interacting without having to worry about time constraints or their other roles.

- It is always worthwhile telling everyone else who works with the person about Intensive Interaction in general, from the start.

- Don't assume you should know all the answers to their questions, but show them where more information is and problem-solve together if they are interested.

INFLUENCING COLLEAGUES IN YOUR GENERAL SETTING

If you have already started using Intensive Interaction and you want to encourage your organisation to use the approach you might consider the following ideas:

- Begin displaying photographs prominently of the person while involved in interactions. Why not create an Intensive Interaction noticeboard that is regularly updated and has pictures of Intensive Interaction, leaflets, newsletters, details of any local regional support group meetings, etc.

- Assemble a dedicated file or fact pack using, for example, Internet resources, a list of references or actual copies of published articles, any other publications or resources you have, such as the Nind and Hewett books, the training DVDs, the Intensive Interaction newsletter, or details of upcoming Intensive Interaction training courses.

- It is very important to involve management. Experience shows that without the support of management, progress will be slow and troublesome, so invite them to look at your Intensive Interaction fact pack and ask for the opportunity to address staff at your next meeting/advertise a meeting of anybody interested/make the resources available/put some information in staff areas/inform parents and carers.

- If you have a meeting (rather than addressing all of your colleagues in one go, which might be a bit of big jump for you) show what video you have and encourage discussion (chocolate biscuits usually help this process) then see whether people are interested in learning more or meeting again to discuss how they might begin working with your person or client.

- Arrange to meet again or to meet regularly to discuss how other people are managing to explore the approach with people in their care.

- If you have not already done so, inform and give information to the parents and/or any other caregivers of those involved in the initiative.

- Strenuously and repeatedly request (or demand!) more formal training.

If things aren't going so well over the course of several sessions

Video is your best and most useful resource. This is especially so if things begin to go wrong in interactions, which although uncommon, does occasionally happen. As has been previously mentioned, the best possible scenario is that you have some video of the person's social responding before you begin using Intensive Interaction. This acts as your baseline. This is valuable evidence because you can look back on it in the weeks and months following, to see where you have come from, or to see what has gone off track. (Note that it is also interesting to compare it with later video, so that you can also reflect on the different means that you come to interact with.)

A less positive scenario is that you have no video (try to get some). Your video is an invaluable learning resource for your personal learning. Watching it will provide insights into how you, the practitioner, are responding, as much as what the person is doing. Video often shows up the opportunities that were missed in interactions and while initial viewings may be painful to watch, try to learn from it and get over it, rather than getting depressed or frustrated. What we mean to do in an interaction is often different to what we end up doing.

While it is worth videoing every interaction that is practicable, real world considerations will probably mean it is only possible to get video every few days. If you cannot video sessions, try to get into the habit of creating a log or some sort of written record of interactions including the 'where?', 'when?', 'what happened?' and 'why you think whatever happened was significant'. Invariably, once you start taking video footage, it seems that the best interactions happen on the days that you don't have the camera set up ready. The only answer is to have a video charged and ready somewhere in your room – that way you will have it to hand and you will get the footage you need to show others.

Taking regular video gives you a record of progress and provides you with evidence to help you to confirm whether there is a problem, or if it is just that the nature of the person's response is changing or elaborating and you have missed the progression.

Individual practitioners sometimes find that being the only person using the approach in their particular setting is causing problems. This usually comes from others' misinterpretation or lack of information about what you are doing. If this is so, be proactive and offer information. When you are trying to involve others, it is usually best to show them video footage of people that they know, which means that it helps to be comfortable when showing video of yourself interacting.

Discussion with your colleagues will always help you to consider how best to apply the principles of the approach to the person concerned. As well as this you will have a 'sounding board' to help you to confirm your suppositions about what is developing, while helping you to reflect on your own interactions as objectively as possible.

If you find yourself unsupported or at a loss for where to go for advice, there are a number of regional support groups that you can attend to develop your practice and Intensive Interaction knowledge further, and to support others to do the same (see www. intensiveinteraction.co.uk).

When you are enthused with an idea or innovation, it is often difficult to identify looming problems until you either find yourself alone or at a precipice. The two most obvious arenas where problems are encountered are:

1. things going wrong within interactions with the person

   If you find that the person seems to be losing interest or motivation to interact, the answer is usually simple – do more observation and/or watch some video of recent interactions. Ensure you are responding in a manner which the person can perceive, and do so at a distance, rate and intensity that pleases them. Most interactive problems arise when the person cannot tell whether what you are doing actually relates to them, or when something you are doing as part of your response causes them to be anxious. Watch video with colleagues to try to identify the problem and resume offering yourself for interaction with this in mind. If the person is aware of you and recognises that you are controllable and reliably responsive, it is quite unusual for them not to want to explore your responses unless you are simply 'too much', 'too close', 'too fast'. Your best scenario is that you are not the only practitioner interacting with the particular person – is your colleague experiencing the same thing?

2. things going wrong with the environment in which you work.

   It is common to want to be able to do more but to be limited by the opportunities open to us:

(a) Rooms are often too small, too crowded or too noisy: can you find a time or place that is less congested? Even though it has been stated that successful Intensive Interaction does not require a discrete or quiet room to be successful, it might be that if the person can't discriminate you from the other events that constantly compete for their attention, it could be best to begin or build up familiarity by interacting in a quieter area, especially if they have a preferred place anyway.

(b) Timetables are too rigid/time is too limited: remember – Intensive Interaction is not a content to be delivered but 'a way' of interacting with the person. Although it is certainly desirable to have regular and sufficient time to commit to longer interactions, you can do Intensive Interaction in any setting, using any 'session' (or gap between sessions) as a context for interaction. All you need to do is to identify what the person is focusing on at that particular moment and then demonstrably join them in their interest, responding encouragingly to any potential interactivity that they show. Your interaction does not need to be formalised in any way. You can interact with the person as they wait for transport home, in lulls between more formal sessions, or at breaktime or recesses. You might start by simply spending the time you would normally have with them, or have to greet them, by joining them in a few moments of their characteristic style of activity, every time you bump into each other.

(c) Colleagues can be problematic: don't forget that for some people who work in services for people with intellectual disabilities what you are doing is challenging. This way of working may be different to the dominant culture you find yourself in. Many people still find it difficult to interact with the degree of friendliness and informality that this approach relies on, and they may be rather discouraging of any 'non-functional' contact. Because good practice looks like play, a critical observer might assume that you are simply imitating or mimicking the person. Don't be defensive; you have a growing body of published, peer-reviewed research which can be used to explain what you are doing. Explain what you are doing and offer them a presentation or discussion.

(d) Age-appropriateness is still an issue: many services for people with intellectual disabilities maintain a rigorous policy requiring all activities to be appropriate to the chronological age of the person rather than the level of development of their cognitive understanding. Others require policy statements for all physical contact. While it is not in the remit of this particular book to re-visit these issues, you might certainly seek the support of the person's parents or carers, or indeed the management of the establishment you work in, by offering information and video examples or requesting that training be made available. Pointing people to the growing body of literature and published research on Intensive Interaction might also be useful.

(e) Behaviour that challenges us or a service is still an issue: if the person has begun to demonstrate aggressive behaviour or behaviour that challenges those around them, try to identify what the person is trying to accomplish by this behaviour and respond – usually challenging behaviour has a clear communicative function – sorry to be repetitive, but it is back to using structured and reflective written and video records.

It is important that if you sense that 'things are not going well', you don't take it personally and that you find help. You could certainly ask for help from more experienced staff or people with more Intensive Interaction experience, to confirm or dispel your anxiety. In any case it is generally good practice to work collaboratively with colleagues as this is much more sustainable than working individually. If you find yourself being a lone practitioner, with no support from colleagues, find support elsewhere in regional networks or via Internet forums.

Finally, as you perform an audit of the things you think are going wrong, also actively look for the good things that are happening – remember to be fair on yourself.

If things are going badly wrong over the course of several sessions

First, define the problem. What is happening differently from what you expected?

Second, don't take it personally; you are doing your best. There may be a number of reasons for things not going well.

Third, get help.

This is where all the effort you made to take regular video throughout your interactions will pay off, because you can review it to identify when any problems emerged. Review the video together with a colleague or someone with more experience of the person or the approach. If you feel the problem might be a personality clash, perhaps you can ask someone else to step in for you and see if they can work more productively. You could perhaps observe them directly or watch any video that they take, to identify significant differences of approach or response.

Finally, if you cannot identify the problem, you might decide to read more books or articles about Intensive Interaction, or go to a training event.

Consider how Intensive Interaction can be used in the longer term, and how this issue is best addressed and organised

The greatest strength of Intensive Interaction is that it has been so well received by the most important people involved with its use – that is, those people with social or communicative impairments and their direct carers. The best way to support the use of Intensive Interaction is to get them involved, and then systematically record and demonstrate the process and any associated progress to as many other people as possible.

At a more systemic level you could ask some insightful questions about yourself, or about the services accessed by the person you are caring for or working with. These questions can be used to establish quickly the extent to which a service appropriately encourages, supports and manages the use of Intensive Interaction. The questions can also be used to identify specific actions that may improve on the current service processes and practices:

- As an Intensive Interaction practitioner, or carer, or parent, or the manager of a service is your level of knowledge about the philosophy and practices of Intensive Interaction sufficient for your current role? If not, what could you do to improve this situation?

- How is your own, or your fellow staff's access to Intensive Interaction knowledge and guidance organised? How do you get Intensive Interaction training, and then move onto further practice development and sustained follow-up support?

- How do you organise practical supervision of your own or colleagues' Intensive Interaction practices? Where do you go for non-judgemental Intensive Interaction advice and guidance?

- Who exactly is, or should be, responsible to ensure Intensive Interaction happens for a particular client, learner or service user? Does one person make sure Intensive Interaction happens regularly, and is recorded and reflected on regularly? If not, how is it managed and can this process be improved?

- How do you structure an individual client's access to Intensive Interaction? Is it integrated into a their normal daily routine or sessionally timetabled at some times during their day? Which way would be best for the person you care for or work with – some combination of them both?

- How do you share knowledge of successful individual client Intensive Interaction strategies or techniques that worked well with the person you work with or care for? Does this involve structured recording and information sharing across the staff team, for example via a specific recording sheet or a strengths and needs plan (SNAP)? See the glossary for further details on the SNAP system.

- Are there any specific policies that you need to have in place regarding aspects of Intensive Interaction practice with individual learners or clients, for example with respect to the possible use of physical contact? Are there any other policies you should have in place?

- How do you share successful individual Intensive Interaction practices with other services that are accessed by your person? These may include, for example, day services, schools, respite care services, etc.

However, generally the most important issue in making Intensive Interaction a continued success will be the resourcefulness and drive of the individual practitioners who use the approach with sensitivity, perseverance and a sound method for supportive and yet critical reflection.

Some other issues worth considering
EVIDENCE OF EFFECTIVENESS

Another means of supporting Intensive Interaction practice is to become familiar with the growing body of evidence indicating its potential to generate increased communication and sociable interactivity. Such evidence comes in its most valid and robust form from Intensive Interaction research studies published in peer reviewed research or academic journals (as indicated in the useful reading section near the end of this book). However, there is also a lot of evidence for the effectiveness of Intensive Interaction that comes from non-research sources, such as other practitioner anecdotes and narrative accounts of their own success (and sometimes failures) of using Intensive Interaction. Such accounts are often useful as evidence of real-life experiences, and as such can help inform your own use of Intensive Interaction.

Given the combination of supportive evidence for Intensive Interaction it readily suggests that effective Intensive Interaction is achievable by very many people with just some basic Intensive Interaction knowledge and support.

PLANNING FOR SUSTAINABILITY OF INTENSIVE INTERACTION

Anyone using Intensive Interaction should prepare and plan for sustainable practice change, and this will require the creation of longer term support mechanisms. These may include:

- having regular access to training opportunities at appropriate intervals (these should be flexible since some people may need more frequent training than others)

- having regular opportunities for positive and constructive peer support and advice

- looking to promote open avenues for communication in Intensive Interaction planning and development which should actively include the opinions of service users (whenever possible), direct carers, support workers and/or family members, involved professionals (e.g. teachers, various therapists, psychologists, or others), and any other significant person who has something worthwhile to contribute

- having the regular availability of well-informed and affirmative leadership, management and supervision (including hands-on modelling of appropriate Intensive Interaction techniques)

- having regular access to new research evidence and relevant literature

- having access to a supportive Intensive Interaction network (within an organisation and/or externally if appropriate).

SUPPORTIVE NETWORKING

A really good way to develop and sustain your Intensive Interaction interventions effectively is to do so with the support and encouragement of a wide group of fellow Intensive Interaction practitioners who share the same goals, and understand the ups and downs of working in this way. Such a group of people can be a mutually supportive network that can act as a sounding-board for people to talk through any difficulties associated with using Intensive Interaction and, equally importantly, they can also be people with whom to share achievements and successes.

It is always much harder to work interactively alone – finding and attending an Intensive Interaction support group (either with colleagues or externally) should provide an understanding and supportive forum. The best way to work is affirmatively and in mutually supportive ways together with other people – very much like doing Intensive Interaction.

CHAPTER 5 What You Might Expect to Come From the Use of Intensive Interaction

The potential outcomes from Intensive Interaction are neither complex nor difficult to understand. Essentially the outcomes of using Intensive Interaction with a person with an intellectual disability or a social or communicative impairment are encompassed in the provision of their very basic human needs (and almost certainly human rights as well). In the broadest sense they are quite simply social acceptance and social inclusion, although through such acceptance and inclusion other beneficial outcomes might well accrue in the longer term.

Looking more specifically, there are several different types of outcome that Intensive Interaction practitioners might be wanting for the person they are working with. Most generally, and most immediately, there is likely to be the aim of increased social engagement or inclusion due to improved or increased sociability and meaningful two-way communication.

If we were to identify the most commonly evidenced communicative gains for the person with a communicative or social impairment then the body of published research indicates increased or novel interactive responses in the following ways:

- increased social initiation and/or engagement (Barber 2008; Cameron and Bell 2001; Kellett 2000, 2003, 2004; Nind 1996; Watson and Fisher 1997)

- increased levels of contingent smiling (Barber 2008; Leaning and Watson 2006; Lovell, Jones and Ephraim 1998; Nind 1996)

- increased levels of eye contact or looking at another person's face (Barber 2008; Cameron and Bell 2001; Kellett 2000, 2003, 2004, 2005; Leaning and Watson 2006; Lovell *et al.* 1998; Nind 1996; Watson and Knight 1991)

- increased levels of socially significant physical contact (Barber 2008; Elgie and Maguire 2001; Firth *et al.* 2008; Kellett 2000, 2003, 2004; Lovell *et al.* 1998)

- increased toleration of, or responsiveness to physical proximity (Firth *et al.* 2008; Nind 1996)

- improved levels of joint attention (Kellett 2000, 2003, 2004, 2005; Leaning and Watson 2006; Lovell *et al.* 1998; Nind 1996)

- increased use of vocalisation (Cameron and Bell 2001; Elgie and Maguire 2001; Kellett 2000; Lovell *et al.* 1998; Watson and Knight 1991).

However, the ultimate aim of the Intensive Interaction practitioner might well be more than just contemporaneous social inclusion and sociable interactivity; the role of the Intensive Interaction might be seen in educational or even therapeutic terms. That does not mean that Intensive Interaction can be seen as some kind of magic bullet or 'cure-all', but it can be used as a means of developing useful and purposeful relationships with someone with a social or communicative impairment. Such relationships can in turn be useful in supporting and facilitating learning in early or fundamental communication abilities (Nind and Hewett 2005).

For some practitioners Intensive Interaction is seen as an approach for reducing social isolation and physical passivity, while equally some practitioners might use Intensive Interaction as a means of gaining a sense of mutuality that might enable a person to control their arousal levels through shared control of a period of interactivity, allowing the practitioner to influence the tempo and stimulation associated with a person's activity.

From another perspective, successful Intensive Interaction can be seen in therapeutic terms, as secure relationships are a key ingredient in securing good mental health (and are demonstrated in some circumstances to be protective against depression and low self-esteem (Berry in Firth *et al.* 2010, p.99)).

Other practitioners have deliberately used Intensive Interaction to address (i.e. to ameliorate or reduce the frequency and degree of) self-stimulatory or self-absorbed activity, and even some kinds of self-injurious behaviour in people with severe or profound and multiple learning disabilities. Intensive Interaction has also been deliberately used to improve communication and sociable interactivity as a means of addressing a person's levels of apparent anxiety or their recourse to challenging behaviour, for example physical aggression, as means of expression (Berry in Firth *et al.* 2010, p.32).

However, although all of the above issues might be addressed for individual participants, and an Intensive Interaction practitioner's major aims might often be very successfully realised by the sustained use of Intensive Interaction, all these things will rely on an Intensive Interaction intervention being carried out with:

- the social and communicative needs of a person with a social or communicative impairment always being at the very centre of any Intensive Interaction intervention

- the person always being a voluntary and willing participant in any Intensive Interaction

- the person being able to lead the interactivity and continuously negotiate and renegotiate its duration, form and tempo with the Intensive Interaction practitioners

- the Intensive Interaction practitioners clearly demonstrating:

  o the necessary sensitivity and responsiveness

  o perseverance in the face of any practical (or other) difficulties

  o the necessary levels of sustained physical, emotional and intellectual effort and intensity

  o collaborative teamworking with other staff or carers, or even other teams of staff or carers o the necessary knowledge of effective 'infant-caregiver' interactional strategies (albeit for some practitioners this being tacit or intuitive procedural knowledge of effective 'infant-caregiver' interactional strategies, i.e. *knowing* how to do it, rather than necessarily being able to talk about or theorise on Intensive Interaction)

o the necessary collaborative and supportive critical reflection on the particular Intensive Interaction strategies used to socially engage the person with a social or communicative impairment

- and finally, carrying through an Intensive Interaction intervention with the necessary involvement of those other people who mainly work with or care for the person, even if they have never even heard of Intensive Interaction – if you are to succeed fully, and do so in the longer term, then you certainly need to engage such people in the processes of Intensive Interaction as well.

So, there it is. Intensive Interaction is not difficult (mainly) but neither is it a gentle stroll in the park. But it is truly worth the effort, and the more effort you put in and the more people you get to join you and help, the easier it will become, and the more certain you will be in providing the people you work with or care for with the kinds of social interactions that they have a right to and deserve. You can be confident that the benefits of their experiences will be substantial.

FURTHER READING

If you now wish to investigate Intensive Interaction further then we would strongly suggest that you read one of the following books, and most certainly read the source material by Melanie Nind and Dave Hewett. Below are some recommended books:

- Firth, G., Berry, R. and Irvine, C. (2010) *Understanding Intensive Interaction: Context and Concepts for Professionals and Families.* London: Jessica Kingsley Publishers.

- Hewett, D. and Nind, M. (1998) *Interaction in Action.* London: David Fulton.

- Kellett, M. and Nind, M. (2003) *Implementing Intensive Interaction in Schools: Guidance for Practitioners, Managers, and Coordinators.* London: David Fulton.

- Nind, M. and Hewett, D. (2001) *A Practical Guide to Intensive Interaction.* Kidderminster: British Institute of Learning Disabilities.

- Nind, M. and Hewett, D. (2005) *Access to Communication,* 2nd edition. London: David Fulton.

- Zeedyk, S. (ed.) (2008) *Promoting Social Interaction for Individuals with Communicative Impairments 'Making contact'.* London: Jessica Kingsley Publishers.

Also, you might like to surf the Internet for further Intensive Interaction information, articles and resources. Some useful websites are:

- www.IntensiveInteraction.co.uk: the 'official' Intensive Interaction website, with sections on 'what is Intensive Interaction?' 'who is Intensive Interaction for?' 'How does Intensive Interaction work – what do you do?' and a variety of other information, features, links and downloadable documents, for example the Intensive Interaction newsletter.

- www.leedspft.nhs.uk/our_services/ld/intensiveinteraction: the Leeds Partnerships NHS Trust (formerly the Leeds Mental Health NHS Trust) Intensive Interaction webpage, with a number of links to downloadable documents, including the latest issue of the Intensive Interaction newsletter, documents on the 'Framework for Recognising Attainment in Intensive Interaction' and the 'Strengths and Needs Analysis and Planning' system.

- www.bild.org.uk/pdfs/05faqs/ii.pdf: where a BILD (*British Institute of Learning Disabilities*) factsheet on Intensive Interaction is available (downloadable as a pdf file). The factsheet has sections on: Why Intensive Interaction? What is Intensive Interaction? When and Where? and Who?

- http://en.wikipedia.org/wiki/Intensive_interaction: a page on Intensive Interaction on Wikipedia, the free Internet encyclopaedia. This page gives some information and background to the approach.

- www.drmarkbarber.co.uk: Dr Mark Barber's webpage. This site has a number of links to downloadable documents (including some Intensive Interaction paperwork resources).

Some of the most informative and influential research papers on Intensive Interaction are as follows:

- Barber, M. (2008) 'Using Intensive Interaction to add to the palette of interactive possibilities in teacher-pupil communication.' *European Journal of Special Needs Education 23,* 4, 393–402.

- Elgie, S. and Maguire, N. (2001) 'Intensive Interaction with a woman with multiple and profound disabilities; a case study.' *Tizard Learning Disability Review, 6,* 3, 18–24.

- Firth, G., Elford, H., Crabbe, M. and Leeming, C. (2008) 'Intensive Interaction as a novel approach in social care: Care staff's views on the practice change process.' *Journal of Applied Research in Intellectual Disabilities 21,* 1, 58–69.

- Kellett, M. (2000) 'Sam's story: Evaluating Intensive Interaction in terms of its effect on the social and communicative ability of a young child with severe learning difficulties.' *Support for Learning 15*, 4, 165–171.

- Kellett, M. (2005) 'Catherine's legacy: Social communication development for individuals with profound learning difficulties and fragile life expectancies.' *British Journal of Special Education 32*, 3, 116–121.

- Leaning, B. and Watson T. (2006) 'From the inside looking out – an Intensive Interaction group for people with profound and multiple learning disabilities.' *British Journal of Learning Disabilities 34*, 2, 103–109.

- Lovell, D., Jones, S. and Ephraim, G. (1998) 'The effect of Intensive Interaction on the sociability of a man with severe intellectual disabilities.' *International Journal of Practical Approaches to Disability 22, 2/3*, 3–8.

- Nind, M. (1996) 'Efficacy of Intensive Interaction; Developing sociability and communication in people with severe and complex learning difficulties using an approach based on caregiver-infant interaction.' *European Journal of Special Educational Needs 11*, 1, 48–66.

- Samuel, J., Nind, M., Volans, A. and Scriven, I. (2008) 'An evaluation of Intensive Interaction in community living settings for adults with profound intellectual disabilities.' *Journal of Intellectual Disabilities 12*, 2, 111–126.

- Watson, J. and Fisher, A. (1997) 'Evaluating the effectiveness of Intensive Interaction teaching with pupils with profound and complex learning disabilities.' *British Journal of Special Education 24*, 2, 80–87.

- Watson, J. and Knight, C. (1991) 'An evaluation of Intensive Interactive teaching with pupils with very severe learning difficulties.' *Child Language Teaching and Therapy 7*, 3, 310–325.

- Zeedyk, M.S., Caldwell, P. and Davies, C.E. (2009) 'How rapidly does Intensive Interaction promote social engagement for adults with profound learning disabilities and communicative impairments?' *European Journal of Special Needs Education 24*, 2, 119–137.

- Zeedyk, S., Davies, C., Parry, S. and Caldwell, P. (2009) 'Fostering social engagement in Romanian children with communicative impairments: Reflections by newly trained practitioners on the use of Intensive Interaction.' *British Journal of Learning Disabilities 37*, 3, 186–196.

Some of the most interesting or significant position papers on Intensive Interaction include the following:

- Barber, M. (2007) 'Imitation, interaction and dialogue using Intensive Interaction: Tea party rules.' *Support for Learning 22*, 3, 124–130.

- Firth, G. (2008) 'A dual aspect process model of Intensive Interaction.' *British Journal of Learning Disabilities 37*, 1, 43–49.

- Irvine, C. (2001) 'On the floor and playing…' *Royal College of Speech and Language Therapy Bulletin*, 9–11 November.

- Kennedy, A. (2001) 'Intensive Interaction.' *Learning Disability Practice 4*, 3, 14–15.

- Nind, M. and Powell, S. (2000) 'Intensive Interaction and autism: Some theoretical concerns.' *Children and Society 14*, 2, 98–109.

- Nind, M. and Thomas, G. (2005) 'Reinstating the value of teachers' tacit knowledge for the benefit of learners: using "Intensive Interaction".' *Journal of Research in Special Educational Needs 5*, 3, 97–100.

- Nind, M. (2000) 'Teachers' understanding of interactive approaches in special education.' *International Journal of Disability, Development and Education 47*, 2, 184–199.

- Samuel, J. (2001) 'Intensive Interaction.' *Clinical Psychology Forum 148*, 22–25.

GLOSSARY

Active learning: a style of working originally developed by Lilli Nielsen (1992) (a Danish preschool teacher and psychologist) to assist young people with visual impairments and 'multiple challenges' to explore their environments, the approach uses 'little rooms' and other experiences to aid learning – for further information see: *An Introduction to Dr Lilli Nielsen's Active Learning* at www.tsbvi.edu/Education/vmi/nielsen.htm.

Agency or 'sense of agency': the understanding that you personally can make things happen, as opposed to having to be a recipient of events or the actions of others.

Augmented mothering: this is the process, as developed by psychologist Dr Geraint Ephraim in the 1980s, of using infant-caregiver type interactions to recreate mothering type activities for people with severe or profound learning disabilities.

Cadence: a particular speed or rhythm of activity (e.g. movements or sounds) or rhythmical pulses or sequences of activity.

Communication partner: one of the people in an interaction.

Community of practice (CoP): a 'community of practice' is generally seen as a group of people who have common concerns or issues, and who collaboratively work together to deepen their understanding and knowledge of their shared interest or interests.

Confirming touch: physical contact given in such a way which affirms, comforts, or acknowledges another person.

Dialogues: a dialogue is a responsive two-way conversation where both people adjust and react to the other's contributions.

Emerging mutual response: emerging mutual responses can be said to be happening as the learner begins to respond to the skilled communication partner's presence, as opposed to the skilled partner simply timing their contribution to fit into the pauses between the pulses in the learner's activity.

Focus of interest: the activity or item which is currently holding the person's attention or interest.

Fundamentals of communication (the): the 'Fundamentals of Communication' or 'fundamental communication abilities' (Nind and Hewett 1994) are identified as the pre-verbal communication behaviours that usually develop before symbolic language (i.e. identifiable words). These Fundamentals of Communication include using eye contact; pre-verbal vocalisations; exchanging facial expansions; physical contact and body language.

Imputing or using intentionality: using 'Intentionality' means deliberately acting as if people are deliberately communicating with you, even if you are not certain that they are. Therefore when interacting you can employ intentionality and respond to people as if they were intentionally trying to communicate with you, even if they aren't really, not yet!

Infant-caregiver interactions: 'infant-caregiver interactions' are the sort of interactions that frequently occur between young infants and their primary caregivers (usually, although by no means exclusively, their parents). Such infant-caregiver interactions are usually mutually enjoyable. They can sometimes be pre-verbal in nature, although they do often involve simple commentaries (on the child's actions), and/or songs and rhymes, and often involve a recognisable use of embellished intonation sometimes called 'Motherese' (see below).

Intellectual radar: 'getting on someone's intellectual radar' is a phrase Mark Barber uses to describe what practitioners are doing when they manage to register in the learner's attention or consciousness, possibly by distracting them from their self-involved activity by standing nearby and using behaviours which they recognise as their own.

Interaction: an 'interaction' in its broadest sense is any kind of mutually recognisable and meaningful two-way communication.

Interactive routines and/or repertoires: as interactive relationships become established, mutually developed interactions often fall into familiar patterns as they are revisited or repeated, and both partners begin to recognise the routines – these idiosyncratic 'routines' or games emerge naturally and although not planned, become recognisable as they happen.

Intuition: the fluid decision-making process that allows people to make snap decisions based on 'how things look'. Intuition is not based on evidence or proof, but often on the apparent human sense of a situation.

Joint focus/joint-focus activities: an activity which is shared by two people and forms a mutually shared focus or centre point for their interactivity or social behaviour.

Motherese: 'Motherese' is a type of communication identified as being used with pre-verbal infants, by adults, and it deploys an embellished or exaggerated intonation to draw and hold the infant's attention. 'Motherese' tends to be used in simple commentaries (on the infant's actions), and when singing songs and rhymes.

Mutual attunement: a subjective feeling of shared familiarity involving matched and interdependent emotional states, usually arrived at through a joint focus or cooperative endeavour.

Non-intimate (areas of the body): parts of the body that prevailing social convention deems admissible to be touched in public.

Observation: 'observation' is the process of objectively looking at what is going on in a certain set of circumstances. Observations are not subjective and individualistic explanations, but independent, impartial and unprejudiced. There should only be one observation of any given situation.

Playfully ritualised exchanges: exchanges between familiar partners can often include mutually recognised and playfully repeated interactive routines. These might be called playfully *ritualised* exchanges as they can (to some observers) seem to be non-functional and unnecessarily recycled. Having a consistent or unvarying way of greeting someone can be seen as ritualised.

Pre-verbal and non-verbal: 'pre-verbal' generally means a type of communication that usually comes before the development of symbolic language (i.e. words and phrases). Therefore pre-verbal communication generally means communication that is non-verbal (or non-symbolic) in nature, for example non-symbolic vocal sounds or gestures, and people who are described as 'pre-verbal' are people who have not yet learned the skills of symbolic speech or understanding.

Profound learning disability (profound intellectual disability): a 'profound learning disability' is an intellectual disability that will profoundly restrict a person's ability even to partially understand many of the events and situations that they encounter, and a person with a profound learning disability will probably not *understand* any words or phrases said to them (although they might *recognise* their own name). Note: the UK term *profound learning disability (or difficulty)* equates with *profound intellectual disability* in other countries.

Pulses of behaviour/activity or pulsing: unless behaviour is consistent and without rest, it has active phases punctuated by periods of inactivity or rest. The active phases which might form rhythmic cycles or routines might also be called pulses of behaviour or activity.

Sense of self: although this is a difficult term to define exactly it generally refers to an individual's views of their own identity and worth – in essence who and what they feel they are in relation to other people in terms of equality or power relations, social acceptance or exclusion, and it can even include issues of gender identity and class.

Sensory channel: the different senses through which we perceive or channel information about our environment, for example touch, vision, hearing, smell, taste, position or movement, with each being seen as a separate channel through which we sense the world around us.

Sensory signature: a 'sensory signature' is a recognisable pattern of sensory stimulation that is used as a greeting to alert someone with a sensory impairment to your presence, for example when working with a blind person using a particular sequence of familiar sounds and/or physical contacts as an introductory greeting.

Severe learning disability: a 'severe learning disability' is an intellectual disability that will severely restrict a person's ability to fully understand many of the events and situations that they encounter – especially any use of symbolic language, that is, words or phrases. Note: the UK term *severe learning disability (or difficulty)* equates with *severe intellectual disability* in other countries.

Skilled partner or more skilled partner: in the context of Intensive Interaction, there are usually two people interacting, one of whom has a severe or profound intellectual disability. The partner who is the more experienced, skilled and fluid communicator is often known as the skilled or more skilled partner. The learner is not wholly unskilled, but within this context might be seen as an apprentice in the processes of communication.

Snap plan: the *Strengths and Needs Analysis and Planning* (SNAP) system is a simple and practical tool for identifying a person's current or potential interactive strengths, and it then defines the kinds of activities required to develop those strengths further. For the purposes of supporting Intensive Interaction, initially 'strength' statements are drawn up, based on the skills and current behavioural repertoire of the person, then the kinds of activities listed as 'needs' are designed to promote active participation and social engagement and thus further develop the person's 'strengths'. For further details see: www. leedspft.nhs.uk/_documentbank/Strengths_and_Needs_SNAP_document__2010.pdf.

Sociable: generally refers to being or acting companionably or sociably with other human beings. A person's sociability refers to both their wish to be sociable, and how to go about trying to make this happen, that is, the extent and range of their social skills.

Social or communicative impairment: such an impairment is a difficulty continuously encountered by an individual in their attempts at communication or social activity with other people. Such impairments can be due to a variety of reasons, including severe or profound learning disabilities, autism, severe physical or sensory impairments, or degenerative conditions in body function or mental capacity.

Stimulation: 'stimulation' generally means something that a person can physically sense (through touch, or visually, or from the sounds or movements that something makes), and it is often associated with 'stimulatory' activities that people in some way find interesting or enjoyable. Some people sometimes create some types of stimulation or 'sensory stimulation' for themselves (if the person has a learning disability it might then be called self-stimulatory, self-involved or stereotyped behaviour), or they may seek it from objects or from other people around them.

Taskless or tasklessness: 'tasklessness' describes a process that is engaged in for its own sake, without any previously defined or premeditated objective in mind. Therefore no set task is completed in a 'taskless' activity, and no predetermined outcome achieved – a 'taskless' activity is simply done for the sake of doing it.

Transactions: in this context, a transaction is another way of describing a communicative exchange.

Vocal intonation: the use of changing or varied pitch of a voice; for example, a person might often raise the pitch of their voice or use a rising vocal intonation at the end of a phrase where the grammatical content is a question, or might lower the pitch as a signal of ending an exchange. Pitch or intonation can be deliberately used to give added meaning and interest to vocal communications.

Vocalisations: 'vocalisations' are sounds that people make with their vocal chords, and for most people outside early infancy, these are generally in the form of words, phrases and sentences, that is, symbolic language. However, vocalisations can also be pre-verbal or non-verbal sounds, and even if these are not recognisable words, they might still be used as a form of communication by people with severe or profound and multiple learning difficulties.

Recording Sheets for Intensive Interaction

Intensive Interaction Sessional Recording Sheet 1

A Framework for Recognising Attainment in *Intensive Interaction*

CLIENT OR LEARNER'S NAME:_____

Date: / /

Encounter: The student or client is present during an interactive episode without any obvious awareness of its progression, *e.g. a willingness to tolerate a shared social atmosphere or environment is sufficient.*	Brief details here:
Awareness: The student or client appears to notice, or fleetingly focus on an event or person involved in the interactive episode, *e.g. by briefly interrupting a pattern of self-absorbed movement or vocalisation.*	Brief details here:
Attention and response: The student or client begins to respond (although not consistently) to what is happening in an interactive episode, *e.g. by showing signs of surprise, enjoyment, frustration or dissatisfaction.*	Brief details here:

Engagement: The student or client shows consistent attention to the interactive episode presented to them, *e.g. by sustained looking or listening, or repeatedly following events with movements of their eyes, head or other body parts.*	Brief details here:
Participation: The student or client engages in sharing or taking turns in a sequence of events during an interactive episode, *e.g. by intentionally sequencing their actions with another person or by intentionally passing signals repeatedly back and forth.*	Brief details here:
Involvement: The student or client makes active efforts to reach out, consistently join in, or even comment in some way on the interaction, *e.g. by sequencing their actions and speaking, signing, vocalising or gesturing in some consistent and meaningful way.*	Brief details here:
Student initiated interaction: The student or client independently starts an interaction (that cannot be described as repetitive or self-absorbed behaviour) and engages another person in the activity with social intent.	Brief details here:
General comments: Any comments here about: • general mood, behaviour, etc. • things that were surprising or exceptional, or • any other comments on interactions.	Brief details here:

The framework is based on the work of S. Aitken and M. Buultjens (1992), E. Brown (1996), and J.M. McInness and J.A. Treffry (1982): see the 'Recognising progress and achievement' section at www.qcda.gov.uk/resources/assets/P_scales_Guidelines.pdf (Qualifications and Curriculum Authority)

Intensive Interaction Sessional Recording Sheet 2

CLIENT OR LEARNER'S NAME:_____

Date:		Client's Name:		Partner's Name:	
Encounter	Awareness	Attention and response	Engagement	Participation	Involvement

Brief description:

Client initiated interactions:

Date:		Client's Name:		Partner's Name:	
Encounter	Awareness	Attention and response	Engagement	Participation	Involvement

Brief description:

Client initiated interactions:

Date:		Client's Name:		Partner's Name:	
Encounter	Awareness	Attention and response	Engagement	Participation	Involvement

Brief description:

Client initiated interactions:

Intensive Interaction Sessional Recording Sheet 3

Client name:	Staff name:	Date:

What happened: (Who started it? How did it start? What game(s) did you play? Where were you?)

Significant events: (Did anything new or unusual happen? Did anything stand out to be remembered or included next time?)

Try to evaluate your performance: (What worked? What didn't? What would you avoid or do differently next time?)

What, for you, was the point? (What do you think was happening?)

Intensive Interaction Sessional Recording Sheet 4

15 minute observation record of_____

Date: /   /   What time is it?

Engagement: Pupil is in 1:1/in group/in parallel/alone undirected/with chosen item.
Context: e.g. on the mats in the corner of the room/facing wall/rocking/alone but watching others/engrossed in his own game/wandering.
Sounds: is s/he making sounds as they move, e.g. rhythmic noises/vocal babble/singing/other?
Vision: where, and at what is s/he looking? Is there eye contact with, or tracking of others? Peers/staff/activities?
Movement: does s/he move rhythmically around the same area or person? Does s/he pick up objects or touch people? Are specific objects or types of object of interest, examined, held, retained?
Touch: what is touched? Is there any pattern in how objects *or* people are greeted, watched, felt, used or played with?
Preferences: what does s/he spend most of their time doing or seem to most enjoy?
Communication: which behaviours seem to be directed at people, what does s/he seem to react to with most interest?
Involvement: which behaviours can you imagine joining in with, what might you do to advertise yourself, or get an invitation to join in?

REFERENCES

Astell, A. and Ellis, M. (2006) 'The social function of imitation in severe dementia.' *Infant and Child Development 15*, 3, 311–319.

Barber, M. (2007) 'Imitation, interaction and dialogue using Intensive Interaction: Tea party rules.' *Support for Learning 22*, 3, 124–130.

Barber, M. (2008) 'Using Intensive Interaction to add to the palette of interactive possibilities in teacher-pupil communication.' *European Journal of Special Needs Education 23*, 4, 393–402.

Barber, M. and Bowen, K. (2009) *Exploring the Envelope of Intensive Interaction.* Melbourne: Intensive Interaction. [DVD]

Berry, R. (2010) 'Relationship Building and Maintenance.' In G. Firth, R. Berry and C. Irvine (eds) *Understanding Intensive Interaction: Context and Concepts for Professionals and Families.* London: Jessica Kingsley Publishers.

Bowen 2007 (personal communication).

Caldwell, P. (2002) *Learning the Language.* Brighton: Pavilion Publishing. [DVD]

Cameron, L. and Bell, D. (2001) 'Enhanced interaction training.' *Working with People who have a Learning Disability 18*, 3, 8–15.

Department of Health (2009) *Valuing People Now: A New Three-Year Strategy for People with Learning Disabilities.* Available at: www.dh.gov.uk/prod_consum_dh/groups/dh_ digitalassets/documents/digitalasset/dh_093375.pdf, accessed on 29 July 2010.

Elgie, S. and Maguire, N. (2001) 'Intensive Interaction with a woman with multiple and profound disabilities; a case study.' *Tizard Learning Disability Review 6*, 3, 18–24.

Ephraim, G. (1986) *A Brief introduction to Augmented Mothering.* Radlett: Harperbury School.

Firth, G. (2008) 'A dual aspect process model of Intensive Interaction.' *British Journal of Learning Disabilities 37*, 1, 43–49.

Firth, G., Berry, R. and Irvine, C. (2010) *Understanding Intensive Interaction: Context and Concepts for Professionals and Families.* London: Jessica Kingsley Publishers.

Firth, G., Elford, H., Leeming, C. and Crabbe, M. (2008) 'Intensive Interaction as a novel approach in social care: Care staff's views on the practice change process.' *Journal of Applied Research in Intellectual Disabilities 21*, 1, 58–69.

Hewett, D. (2006) *Intensive Interaction DVD.* Dave Hewett, UK [DVD]

Hewett, D. and Nind, M. (1998) *Interaction in Action.* London: David Fulton.

Irvine, C. (2001) 'On the floor and playing…' *Royal College of Speech and Language Therapy Bulletin*, 9–11 November.

Irvine, C. (2010) 'Issues Associated with Personal Characteristics.' In G. Firth, R. Berry and C. Irvine (eds) *Understanding Intensive Interaction: Context and Concepts for Professionals and Families.* London: Jessica Kingsley Publishers.

Kellett, M. (2000) 'Sam's story: Evaluating intensive interaction in terms of its effect on the social and communicative ability of a young child with severe learning difficulties.' *Support for Learning 15*, 4, 165–171.

Kellett, M. (2003) 'Jacob's journey: Developing sociability and communication in a young boy with severe and complex learning difficulties using the Intensive Interaction teaching approach.' *Journal of Research in Special Educational Needs 3*, 1, 1–8.

Kellett, M. (2004) 'Intensive Interaction in the inclusive classroom: using interactive pedagogy to connect with students who are hardest to reach.' *Westminster Studies in Education 27*, 2, 175–188.

Kellett, M. (2005) 'Catherine's legacy: Social communication development for individuals with profound learning difficulties and fragile life expectancies.' *British Journal of Special Education 32*, 3, 116–121.

Kellett, M. and Nind, M. (2003) *Implementing Intensive Interaction in Schools: Guidance for Practitioners, Managers, and Coordinators.* London: David Fulton.

Leaning, B. and Watson T. (2006) 'From the inside looking out – an Intensive Interaction group for people with profound and multiple learning disabilities.' *British Journal of Learning Disabilities 34*, 2, 103–109.

Lovell, D., Jones, R. and Ephraim, G. (1998) 'The effect of Intensive Interaction on the sociability of a man with severe intellectual disabilities.' *International Journal of Practical Approaches to Disability 22*, 2/3, 3–8.

Nielsen, L. (1992) *Space and Self.* Copenhagen: Sikon Press.

Nind, M. (1996) 'Efficacy of Intensive Interaction: Developing sociability and communication in people with severe and complex learning difficulties using an approach based on caregiver-infant interaction.' *European Journal of Special Needs Education 11*, 1, 48–66.

Nind, M. (2000) 'Teachers' understanding of interactive approaches in special education.' *International Journal of Disability, Development and Education 47*, 2, 184–199.

Nind, M. and Hewett, D. (1994) *Access to Communication: Developing the Basics of Communication with People with Severe Learning Difficulties Through Intensive Interaction.* London: David Fulton.

Nind, M. and Hewett, D. (2001) *A Practical Guide to Intensive Interaction.* Kidderminster: British Institute of Learning Disabilities.

Nind, M. and Hewett, D. (2005) *Access to Communication: Developing the Basics of Communication with People with Severe Learning Difficulties Through Intensive Interaction,* second edition. London: David Fulton.

Nind, M. and Powell, S. (2000) 'Intensive Interaction and autism: some theoretical concerns.' *Children and Society 14*, 2, 98–109.

Nind, M. and Thomas, G. (2005) 'Reinstating the value of teachers' tacit knowledge for the benefit of learners: Using Intensive Interaction.' *Journal of Research in Special Educational Needs 5*, 3, 97–100.

Qualifications and Curriculum Authority (2001) *Planning, Teaching and Assessing the Curriculum for Pupils with Learning Difficulties: General Guidelines.* London: QCA Publications. Available at www.qcda.gov.uk/resources/assets/P_scales_Guidelines.pdf, accessed on 28 July 2010.

Samuel, J. (2001) 'Intensive Interaction.' *Clinical Psychology Forum 148,* 22–25.

Samuel, J., Nind, M., Volans, A. and Scriven, I. (2008) 'An evaluation of Intensive Interaction in community living settings for adults with profound intellectual disabilities.' *Journal of Intellectual Disabilities 12,* 2, 111–126.

Seligman, M. (1992) *Helplessness: On Depression, Development and Death.* San Francisco, CA: Freeman.

Watson, J. and Fisher, A. (1997) 'Evaluating the effectiveness of Intensive Interaction teaching with pupils with profound and complex learning disabilities.' *British Journal of Special Education 24,* 2, 80–87.

Watson, J. and Knight, C. (1991) 'An evaluation of Intensive Interactive teaching with pupils with very severe learning difficulties', *Child Language Teaching and Therapy 7,* 3, 310–325.

Zeedyk, S., Davies, C., Parry, S. and Caldwell, P. (2009) 'Fostering social engagement in Romanian children with communicative impairments: Reflections by newly trained practitioners on the use of Intensive Interaction.' *British Journal of Learning Disabilities 37,* 3, 186–196.

INDEX

achievement
   familiar clients 67–8,
      73, 83, 104–5
   unfamiliar clients 66–7,
      72–3, 83, 103–4
acknowledgement 42, 46,
   72, 73
activities 13, 22, 23, 31,
   93
   joint-focus activities 32,
      35, 35, 107
   tempo 48, 49, 51, 67,
      72, 79
   timing 33
   varying activities 70–2
age-appropriateness 127
anticipation 45, 93
anxiety 23, 26–7, 30, 42,
   43, 47, 48, 51, 97,
   135
   recognizing 52, 59, 61,
      64–5
approaching clients 26–7
   familiar clients 29–30,
      57–8, 99–100
   unfamiliar clients 28–9,
      55–6, 96–9
arousal 67, 134
   over-arousal 52, 61, 72
assessment of progress
   familiar clients 88–9,
      113
   unfamiliar clients 86–8,
      112–13
Astell, A. 14
attention 13, 39–40, 63,
   134
attunement 29, 62, 111
augmented mothering 12

Australia 16, 121
autistic spectrum disorder
   11, 14, 46, 50, 119
availability 40, 43, 48, 51,
   56, 67, 103

backing off 43
Barber, M. 121, 133, 134
behaviour 13, 28–9, 39
   challenging behaviour
      23, 72, 88, 112, 119,
      127, 135
   observation 61–2,
      100–3
   self-injurious behaviour
      74–5, 119, 135
Bell, D. 133, 134
Berry, R. 15, 135
blind clients 27–8
body language 52
boredom 33, 36–7, 42,
   61, 70
   recognizing 75–6,
      77–9
Bowen, K. 26, 121
breathing patterns 32, 41,
   48, 60, 61
burst-pause 40–1, 43–4,
   80, 82, 93, 108, 113

cadence 25, 58
Caldwell, P. 26, 121
Cameron, L. 133, 134
carers 9, 15, 23, 24, 36,
   55, 123, 128, 129
   information 123, 127
   planning 131
   repetition 70–1

teamworking 135
use of resource items
   109
challenging behaviour
   23, 72, 88, 112, 119,
   127, 135
children 14, 36, 84
colleagues 16, 20, 44, 54,
   69, 84, 85, 92, 93
   colleagues working in
      same setting 122–3
   colleagues working with
      you 120–2
   less successful sessions
      125, 126–8
common ground 11, 21,
   22, 28, 29, 39, 65
communication partners
   11, 111
   role 94–5
communicative impairment
   9, 11, 63, 97, 98–9,
   103–4, 113, 128
   repetition 70–1
companionship 32–3
competence 115–17
   handling problems
      119–20
   overcoming difficulties
      118
confirming touch 44
connectedness 14, 15
conversation 11, 12, 13,
   19, 24, 27, 31–2,
   65, 66
   burst-pause 40–1
   initiating 65, 66
creativity 74, 81–2

day services 16, 130
defensive reactions 21, 27,
    51, 52
dementia 14
Department of Health 104
developing interactions
    68, 100
    familiar clients 80–2
    unfamiliar clients 79–81
dialogues 28, 42, 60
    burst-pause 40–1
Dictaphones 91
discomfort 59, 63, 95
disengagement 61,
    110–12
    familiar clients 86
    unfamiliar clients 85–6
distractions 20, 25, 50–1,
    54, 55–6, 76, 81, 85,
    87, 96, 110, 112
    resource items 34, 36,
    82
distress 51, 52, 65

echoing 41–2, 93
educational support staff
    16
Elgie, S. 134
Ellis, M. 14
emerging mutual response
    32–3
emotions 58, 59, 93
    emotional connection
    14
engagement 11, 50–1, 61,
    67, 72, 105, 133
    approaching clients 28
    disengagement 61,
    85–6, 111
    familiar clients 43–6,
    52–3, 93–4
    unfamiliar clients
    39–43, 51–52, 91–3
enjoyment 13, 17, 22, 29,
    33, 42, 65, 102, 121
    games 44, 46
    interactions 73, 76, 77,
    82, 84–5, 88

environments 21, 25, 54,
    126
Ephraim, G. 133
epilepsy 53
excitement 25, 52, 64
expectations 66, 67, 68
eye contact 13, 19, 24,
    27, 47, 48, 49, 57,
    61, 80, 97, 100, 134

facial expressions 13, 24,
    40, 42, 46, 48, 56,
    61, 78
facial signalling 92, 100
families 15, 92, 93, 104,
    113, 131
fatigue see tiredness
feedback 16, 67, 89
    feedback from clients
    49, 61, 64, 68, 73,
    75, 98
fellow practitioners 16,
    129, 131
Firth, G. 15, 75, 106,
    134, 135
Fisher, A. 133
focus 25, 26, 39, 59–60,
    61, 72, 80
following client's lead
    64, 78
    familiar clients 65–6
    unfamiliar clients 64–5
formats 31
Framework for
    Recognising
    Attainment in
    Intensive Interaction
    102–3
'friends' 69
fun 41, 44, 68, 79, 112
fundamentals of
    communication 12,
    13, 14, 15, 46, 134

games 31, 41, 44, 46, 58,
    94, 98
    anticipation 45

balls 36
interactive sequences
    62–3, 64
    resource items 82–3,
    108
'good face' 40, 43

hand washing 25–6, 37
health concerns 25
hearing impairment 20,
    27, 41
    approaching clients
    28, 56
Hewett, D. 11, 13, 14, 48,
    91, 121, 123
hygiene 25–6, 37

imitation 39, 41, 44, 82,
    93, 113
indifference 42, 48
Individual Educational
    Plans (IEPs) 17
infancy 14
infant-caregiver
    interactions 12, 136
infections 25–6
insight 9–10, 28, 58,
    65, 83
    colleagues 16, 120
    personal behaviour 93,
    124, 129
intellectual disability 14,
    42, 58, 65, 77, 113,
    133
intellectual radar 27, 44,
    72
Intensive Interaction
    9–10, 84, 135–6
    collaboration with
    clients' others 15–17
    definition 11–12
    evidence of effectiveness
    130–1
    information and
    research 117, 120–1,
    122–3, 127, 130

less successful sessions 117–18, 123–8
observed sessions 30
outcomes 133–6
planning for sustainability 131
potential benefits 13–14, 14–15
promoting 121–23, 128–30
successful sessions 115–17, 120–3
supervision 118
supportive networking 132
unsuccessful sessions 119–20, 128
intentionality 13
interaction 9
interests 11, 12, 22, 28, 65, 69, 108
intrigue 26, 40, 48, 52, 60, 62, 63, 66, 69, 82–3
intuition 58, 71, 81, 98, 113, 136
invitation 27, 43, 52, 53, 59, 97–8
involvement 13, 14, 29, 72, 73, 88, 107
Framework for Recognising Attainment 102–3
Irvine, C. 75
isolation 14, 33, 87, 134

joint-focus activities 34, 35, 107
Jones, S. 133

Kellett, M. 133, 134
Knight, C. 134

Leaning, B. 133, 134
learned helplessness 77

learning disability see intellectual disability; profound learning disability; severe learning disability
leaving 32, 33, 52, 84–5
disengagement 85–6
Lovell , D. 133, 134

Maguire, N. 134
mental handicap see intellectual disability
mental health 87, 134–5
mirroring 23, 39, 61, 70
self-injurious behaviour 74–5
unfamiliar clients 74
mobility 20–1
mood assessment 23, 24, 52, 53, 55, 68, 87, 95, 99, 105, 110
music therapists 17

networks 16, 117, 121, 127, 131
clients 17
supportive networking 132
Nind, M. 11, 13, 14, 48, 62, 91, 123, 133, 134
notes 33, 91

objects of interest see resource items
observation 9
assessing responses 69–70
behaviour 61–2, 100–3
client's mobility 20–1
client's preferred places 19–20
familiar clients 24–5, 49–50, 106–7
unfamiliar clients 21–4, 46–9, 105–6

what to look for 58–9, 59–60, 60–4
occupational therapists 17
optimism 31, 53, 99, 104, 105, 118
organisations 122–3
outcomes 133–6
over-arousal 52, 61, 72

pallor 48, 100
parents 9, 15, 123, 127, 129
patterns of behaviour 72, 92
patterns of response 28, 46, 53, 72, 101
personal space 13, 26–7, 47, 51, 97, 98
backing off 43
physical contact 47, 48, 61, 93, 98–9, 127, 130, 134
physical disability 23
place 19–20
Plato 9
playfully ritualised exchanges 29, 60
playthings see resource items
pleasure 13, 23, 28, 42, 49, 52, 58, 72, 73, 79, 101, 113
recognizing 59, 60
pre-intentional communication 58
pre-verbal vocalisations 61
professional development 117
profound learning disability 11, 12, 14, 58, 119, 135
proximity 19–20, 21, 24, 32, 43, 47, 48, 97, 98–9, 100, 134
psychologists 17, 131
pulses of behaviour 40, 41

recognition 27, 43, 65, 73, 83, 107
record keeping 33, 91, 96, 101
refer/echo 41–2, 44
reflection 9, 10, 63–4, 66–7, 82, 87, 89
  achievement 103–5
  approaching clients 96–100
  assessment of progress 112–13
  disengagement 110–11
  engagement 91–5
  observation 105–7
  resource items 107–9
  timing 95–6, 109–10
relationships 14–15, 71, 73, 134–5
repertoires 24, 29, 32, 43, 44, 46, 49, 56, 79, 101, 112
  conversation 65, 66
  enjoyment of repetition 72
  games 45
  patterns of behaviour 72, 98, 106, 112
  playful ritualisation 60
  resource items 82
repetition 42, 58, 68, 70–1
resource items 32, 33, 36–7, 78, 107–9
  familiar clients 35–6, 82–3
  unfamiliar clients 34–5, 82
respite services 15, 130
routines 28, 29, 32, 43, 58, 101, 108
  development 68
  sabotage 94
  variation 71

sabotage 45, 68, 94, 113
safety considerations 21, 25, 54

schools 13–14, 16, 20, 130
self-injurious behaviour 74–5, 119, 135
Seligman, M. 77
sensory behaviours 42
sensory channels 41
sensory impairment 14
sensory signature 27, 56
severe communicative impairment 9, 11, 14, 77
severe learning disability 11, 12, 14, 77, 117, 135
skilled partners 11, 22
  'good face' 40
  role 28, 29–30, 60
slight adjustment 42
smiling 27, 29, 42, 46, 53, 60, 94, 133
SNAP plan 130
sociability 14, 113, 133
social agency 14, 28, 46, 78
social impairment 9, 11, 14, 63, 97, 98–9, 103–4, 128
  repetition 70–1
social inclusion 14, 15, 17, 22, 113, 133, 134
speech and language therapists 17
stimulation 13, 36, 79, 134
  self-stimulation 14, 135
Strengths and Needs Analysis and Planning see SNAP plan

tasklessness 13
teachers 9, 12, 16, 30, 131
themes 42, 62, 71, 73, 108
therapists 9, 17, 131
timing 30–1, 53–5, 126

familiar clients 32–3, 85, 96, 108
unfamiliar clients 31–2, 84–5, 95–6, 109–10
tiredness 30, 63, 85, 95
tooth grinding 39, 41
touch 22, 40, 42, 72
toys see resource items
training 116, 121, 123, 131
transactions 42, 72
trust 65, 71, 93

UK 104, 121
unexpected occurrences 68–9

videos 33, 52, 69, 70, 76, 101
  assessment of progress 87, 89, 92, 93, 96
  developing competence 116
  influencing colleagues 121–2
  less successful sessions 123–4
  observation 105–6, 107
  unsuccessful sessions 128
visual impairment 20, 41
  approaching clients 27–8, 56
vocal intonation 40
vocalisations 13, 25, 47, 48, 57, 70, 74, 75, 92, 93, 94, 134
  pre-verbal vocalisations 61

Watson, J. 133
Watson, T. 133, 134
wheelchair users 21, 33, 56, 59

Zeedyk, S. 14